Theology in Context

Theology in Context

A Case Study in the Philippines

Dave Johnson

Foreword by Russ Turney

WIPF & STOCK · Eugene, Oregon

Wipf and Stock Publishers
199 W 8th Ave, Suite 3
Eugene, OR 97401

Theology in Context
A Case Study in the Philippines
By Johnson, Dave and Turney, Russ
Copyright©2013 APTS Press
ISBN 13: 978-1-5326-3397-3
Publication date 5/31/2017
Previously published by APTS Press, 2013

This edition is published by Wipf and Stock Publishers under license from APTS Press.

AUTHOR'S PREFACE

All theology is theology in context (Flemming 2005). From the biblical writers onward, all theology is written with a particular worldview in mind. From the subjects with which the biblical authors dealt, as well as the ones which they omitted, their writings reflects the context of their intended audience. The theologians that followed them have done the same throughout church history. The various creeds, for example, reflect the theological milieu in which they were written. Reformation theology, for example, reflects the life and times of Medieval Europe. The list is endless. Western theology, particularly from America, dominates the current scene, at least in the Philippines.

The question, then, is not so much as whether theology is written in context, but which context does it reflect? When theology written for one context crosses cultural boundaries some issues important to the receptor culture are not deal with, while other issues, important as they may be in the sending culture, are not important to the receptors. The situation in the Philippines, where my wife and I live and serve, is a case in point. Virtually every textbook used in the theological training institutions that I know of here comes from the West and reflects that point of view.

A couple of examples will suffice. In nearly 20 years I have served in the Philippines, I have yet to meet a Filipino atheist, making the arguments for the existence of God, which are critical in the Western context, wasted ink. On the other hand, when I was writing my doctoral dissertation, of which this is this book is the published version, I consulted my Bible college systematic theology textbook to see if it dealt with what the Bible has to say about the dead coming back to life—which is a big issue here. Not surprisingly, nothing was mentioned except for the resurrection of Jesus. Sadly, most Filipino writers and missionaries working here have also not engaged this and similar issues to any great degree, at least not in writing. Most of the contextual theology here has been done from a Roman Catholic perspective. In my opinion, there is a critical need for the scholars and writers within the evangelical community to write on the biblical issues relevant to this context. This book is my own modest attempt to contribute to that effort.

As always I would be glad to hear from you. You can contact me through our website, www.daveanddebbiejohnson.com or my blogspot, www.drdavejohnson.blogspot.com.

Dave Johnson, D-Miss
Daraga, Albay, Philippines

October, 2012

ACKNOWLEDGMENTS

If this book is readable at all, it is so because of my wife, Debbie's, patient and thorough editing. To her I am deeply thankful. I would also like to express my gratitude to Dr. Kay Foundation of the Asia Pacific Theological Seminary (APTS) for approving this project to be published by the APTS Press. My thanks also go to all of those who helped in any way with the original doctoral dissertation from which this is drawn. Since they were thanked by name in the acknowledgments of the dissertation itself, I shall not repeat their names here. My thanks also go to Jhen Arro, who did the copy editing, and to my friends at ICI Ministries in Manila, who did the layout and cover design.

More than anyone else, however, I am thankful to Jesus for giving life purpose and for allowing Debbie and I to have had so many wonderful years of ministry in the Philippines. I hope we have many more.

DEDICATION

To Debbie, my beloved wife and soul mate.
God gave me his best when he gave you to me.

FOREWORD

Dave Johnson and I first met around 30 years ago when he was a student at Central Bible College in Springfield, Missouri and I was serving as Youth Director for the Southern Missouri District of the Assemblies of God USA. Later we connected in the Philippines, where we had moved to begin our missionary career and he began making short term evangelism trips. There we saw Dave grow in his vision for missions, his evangelistic ministry and his spiritual life. He eventually moved to the Philippines in 1994 where he met Debbie, his wife, and they have continued serving effectively there since that time. Their ministry continued to expand as they led a Bible School, planted churches, and served as mission coordinator for a large team in the Philippines. Dave also completed a doctoral program and led a team that translated the Full Life Study Bible (aka Fire Bible) notes and articles into the Tagalog and later Cebuano languages of the Philippines. This Full Life Study Bible is used regularly by several thousand pastors and church leaders in various denominations and church groups across the country. It is one of the leadership tools which have profoundly helped the Church understand the Holy Spirit and know how essential He is to our spiritual life.

If those accomplishments were not enough, Dave wrote his first book *Led By the Spirit: The History of the American Assemblies of God Missionaries in the Philippines*. Others had talked about doing this, but his proactive approach to life determined that it was time to take action and an excellent book was the result. We have seen Dave's writing skills continue to sharpen and influence others on a broader level. His commitment to excellence has inspired him to write articles on topics like leadership, spiritual disciplines, setting and reaching goals, discipleship and vision. He is always pushing himself to do better and by example inspires others to follow.

Now, he has written this second book. *Theology in Context: A Case Study in the Philippines* is actually the publication of Dave's doctoral dissertation and is a serious reflection on some of the formal and animistic practices of Catholicism that have resulted in Folk Catholicism. His purpose, after many years of research and reflection, is to offer a biblical response to these practices as well as to the worldview that underpins them. Read, be inspired, and come to a deeper understanding of how the Word of God can and must impact Filipino culture.

Dr. J. Russell Turney
Asia Pacific Regional Director
Assemblies of God (USA) World Missions

LIST OF TABLES

Table 2.1	Methods Used	27
Table 2.2	Subjects Taught or Recommended	33
Table 5.1	A Comparison of Waray and Biblical Cosmologies	70
Table 6.1	To Whom Do You Pray For Help in Times of Drought and Typhoon?	87
Table 6.2	To Whom Do the AG Pray For Help in Times of Drought and Typhoon?	88
Table 6.3	Actions Done Instead of Rituals	90
Table 6.4	To Whom Do They Pray in Times of Trouble?	91
Table 6.5	To Whom Does the AG Pray in Times of Trouble?	93
Table 6.6	Why the AG Prays to Supernatural Beings	94
Table 7.1	Reasons for Going to the Gravesite on All Saints' Day	108
Table 7.2	AG Reasons for Going to the Gravesite on All Saints' Day	109
Table 7.3	Reasons For Not Going to the Gravesite on All Saints' Day	110
Table 7.4	Reasons For Going to the Fiesta	115
Table 7.5	AG Reasons For Going to the Fiesta	117
Table 7.6	Reasons For Not Going to the Fiesta	118
Table 7.7	Reasons Why AG People Do Not Go to the Fiesta	119
Table 8.1	Beliefs Regarding Causes of Sickness	131
Table 8.2	AG Beliefs Regarding Causes of Sickness	133
Table 8.3	Beliefs About Who Can Heal People	139
Table 8.4	AG Beliefs About Who Can Heal People	141
Table 9.1	Beliefs on How to Protect Oneself From Evil Spirits	149
Table 9.2	AG Beliefs on How to be Protected From Evil Spirits	151
Table 9.3	Perceived Results of Demon Possession	157
Table 10.1	Crop Failure	168
Table 10.2	The Holy Spirit	170
Table 10.3	Healing	173
Table 10.4	Why the Waray Came to Christ	174

GLOSSARY OF TERMS

Assemblies of God Church Member: A baptized adult believer who was at least 20 years old who was attending an Assemblies of God church at the time of the field research.

Assemblies of God Population (AG): Members and adherents of Assemblies of God churches that were selected for participation in the field research.

Contextual Theology: Presenting the Good News of Jesus Christ to the Waray people within their own cultural context and worldview without compromising the message in the process.

Folk Catholicism: A mixture animistic beliefs and practices with formal Roman Catholicism, so as to form an essentially different religion (Schumaker 1984:251).

General Population: Waray people living in the *barangays* that were selected for participation in the field research.

Religious Belief: A system of convictions concerning the supernatural that are held by a certain group of people.

Adherent: (or sympathizer in the Philippines) An adult or young person that has shown interest in an Assemblies of God church through attending church services or a Bible study who may or may not be born again and has not yet become a baptized member of the church.

Tambalan: A generic Waray term for herbalist, faith healer, spiritist and witchdoctor.

Waray or Waray people: In this study, this refers to the Waray population at large, which encompasses both the GP and the AG sample populations.

TABLE OF CONTENTS

i	Author's Preface
iii	Acknowledgments
iv	Dedication
v	Foreword
vii	List of Tables
viii	Glossary of Terms
1	**INTRODUCTION**
1	Background
4	Information Needed to Answer the Research Questions
5	Sources of Information
6	Scope and Limitations of the Study
9	**CHAPTER ONE: HISTORY AND DEVELOPMENT OF THE ASSEMBLIES OF GOD IN THE WARAY REGION**
10	The First Period (1960-1972)
15	The Second Period (1972-1988)
22	The Third Period (From 1988 Onward)
25	**CHAPTER TWO: METHODS, MESSAGE AND MIRACLES**
27	The Evangelistic Methods Used
32	The Message: Subject Taught or Recommended
37	The Role of Miracles
41	**CHAPTER THREE: WARAY CULTURE AND WORLDVIEW**
42	Waray Culture
45	Waray Religious Worldview
46	Cosmology

47	Causality
48	Catholic Folk Practices
54	Rituals and Their Roles Among the Waray
59	**CHAPTER FOUR: WARAY RELIGIOUS PRACTITIONERS AND THEIR ROLES**
59	Sorcerers and Their Roles
60	*Tambalans* and Their Roles
69	**CHAPTER FIVE: INTRODUCTION OF THE THEOLOGICAL AND CONTEXTUALIZATION ISSUES**
69	Theological Issues
69	Theological Issues Related to Waray Cosmology
74	Theological Issues Related to Christology
78	Theological Issues Related to Religious Practitioners
83	Contextualization Issues
83	Cultural Dynamics
84	The Worldview Model of Contextualization
87	**CHAPTER SIX: QUESTIONS RELATED TO NATURE AND PRAYER IN TIMES OF NEED**
87	Prayer in Times of Drought and Typhoon
89	Before You Plant Crops, Do You Have a Witchdoctor or Someone Else Come and Perform Rituals or Sacrifices?
91	A Question About Prayer in Time of Need
95	What Does the Bible Say?
95	Providence
98	Blessing and Cursing
99	Divination
101	Spiritual Mediation
107	**CHAPTER SEVEN: QUESTIONS RELATED TO ROMAN CATHOLICISM**
107	Do You Go to the Gravesite on All Saints' Day?

111	What Does the Bible Say?
114	Do You Attend the Town or Barrio Fiesta?
117	Those Who Don't Go to the Fiesta
119	What Does the Bible Say?

131	**CHAPTER EIGHT: QUESTIONS ABOUT SICKNESS AND HEALING**
131	Causes of Sickness According to the Waray
134	What Does the Bible Say?
139	Sources of Healing According to the Waray
142	What Does the Bible Say?

149	**CHAPTER NINE: QUESTIONS ABOUT EVIL SPIRITS**
149	How Do You Protect Yourself From Evil Spirits?
151	What Does the Bible Say?
157	Can People Become Controlled by an Evil Spirit?
158	What Does the Bible Say?

165	**CHAPTER TEN: HOW THE ASSEMBLIES OF GOD WERE TRANSFORMED BY THE GOSPEL**
165	The Doctrine of Salvation
168	Before and After Assessment Regarding Crop Failure
169	Before and After Assessment Regarding the Spirits of the Dead
170	Before and After Assessment Regarding the Holy Spirit
173	Before and After Assessment Regarding Healing
174	Key Elements in Coming to Christ

177	**CHAPTER ELEVEN: CONCLUSIONS AND RECOMMENDATIONS**
177	Missiological Implications Drawn From Kraft's Worldview Model
177	Explanation
178	Evaluation

179	Psychological Reinforcement
180	Integration
183	Adaptation
184	Hypothesis Proven
185	Answering the Research Questions
185	What are the Religious Beliefs of the Waray as They Pertain to Their Animistic Practices?
185	What Were the Elements of the Gospel That Contributed to the Growth and Development of the Assemblies of God Churches Among the Waray?
187	What Comparisons Might be Made Between Biblical Theology and the Religious Belief System of the Waray?
188	Recommendations For Further Study
188	Recommendations For Practical Ministry
191	Recommendations For Broader Application of the Results of This Study
191	Conclusion

Introduction

The claim made by many that the Philippines is a Christian nation is, at best, only partially true. The reality, as many anthropologists, sociologists and theologians familiar with the Philippine context have attested, is that the animistic practices that predated the arrival of Roman Catholicism continue unabated. From burying good luck charms under one's house to consulting witchdoctors for healing, the average Filipino's daily activity reflects a deeply ingrained indigenous consciousness which bears little resemblance to biblical Christianity. Over the last 400 years Roman Catholicism has impacted and changed many of the practices, but the animistic worldview that underpins them remains largely unchallenged.

My purpose in this book is to first understand, respect, explain and engage this worldview while comparing it to biblical revelation. I intend to show how Christians can impact this worldview through an explanation and demonstration of the gospel of Jesus Christ to the Filipino within their cultural context. I will accomplish this through studying a particular people group, the Waray of Leyte and Samar. According to most scholars, their cultural similarities with the rest of the lowland people groups outweigh the differences, making the results of this study broadly applicable.

Background

My initial interest in the Waray people themselves dates back to 1989 when I heard of their need for the gospel while listening to live radio reports from the Lausanne Congress that took place in Manila that year. The Waray were described as one of the most unreached people groups in the Philippines at that time. While the situation has improved somewhat, the need continues to be great. I first visited the Waray region in 1992 during a brief evangelistic tour. From 1994-2001, I then spent a fairly significant amount of time among the Waray, ministering as opportunities were presented and writing a master's thesis on their pagan religious practices (Johnson 2000). That research provided part of the background for this study, focusing on the activities of the various witch doctors and sorcerers. It also suggested potential bridges to the gospel from the Waray point of view. These potential bridges include a basic concept of God, divine healing, Christ as mediator and signs and wonders, all of which were looked at more in depth in the research presented in this text.

The goal of this research is to study the worldview and religious beliefs of the Waray people as well as the growth of the Assemblies of God in this region to identify the elements that could be of value in presenting the gospel in a contextually effective manner. The rationale for studying the Assemblies of God was because my commitment as a missionary with that organization is to its growth and development here in the Philippines.

Another reason for studying the Waray was that, to the best of my knowledge, no such contextual theology, liberal or conservative, currently exists. There are Catholic scholars who have written from a pan-Filipino perspective. While these were helpful and were used in this study, they were written from a point of view that calls for cultural accommodation rather than transformation through the power of the Word of God. The body of literature from an Evangelical and Pentecostal perspective that engages the animistic worldview in the Philippines is small indeed. My hope is that this book will contribute to this field.

The development of a contextual theology is important as it provides for the opportunity to express the unchanging Good News of Jesus Christ within the worldview of the people, making it easier for the Waray to understand God's revelation and to make an informed decision as to whether or not they will become followers of Jesus Christ.

The Waray live on the islands of Leyte and Samar in the eastern Visayan region of the Philippines. They are mostly an agricultural people, growing rice, maize, and many root crops. The 2000 census revealed a regional population of 3,250,195. This does not include Southern Leyte, which is a mainly Cebuano region.

To accomplish the purposes of this study, a number of steps were involved. The backdrop of the Waray culture and worldview was reviewed, based on the literature available, in order to better understand Waray religious values. From the literature, two questionnaires were developed to study the Waray religious belief system. Each question was keyed to a related theological issue. Interviews were also conducted with the pioneer Assemblies of God pastors in the region in order to study the growth and development of the Assemblies of God. The results of the research, along with the literature, were then compared to what the Bible teaches about each theological issue. Missiological principles drawn from Charles Kraft's (1979:54-57) worldview model of contextualization completed the study in chapter eleven.

A contextual theology, then, is a theology that presents the gospel of Jesus Christ within the worldview of the people while being faithful to the Scriptures. In other words, it is communicated in a way in which people will understand and will not seem foreign to them. In doing so, it validates what is biblical in the Waray culture, allows what is not unbiblical and seeks to transform at a deep level that which falls short of biblical revelation. This study intends to assist in this process.

To achieve the goals of the study, three questions were addressed:

- What are the religious beliefs of the Waray as they pertain to their animistic or folk Catholic practices?
- What were the elements of the gospel that contributed to the growth and development of the Assemblies of God churches among the Waray?
- What comparisons might be made between biblical theology and the religious belief system of the Waray?

The study was also undertaken with the following hypotheses: (1) that the religious beliefs of the Waray are steeped in animism and folk Catholicism, (2) the Assemblies of God grew and developed by preaching the gospel, accompanied by demonstrations of the power of God in healing and deliverance from demonic powers, and (3) that contact points can be drawn between the Waray belief system and biblical revelation that will enable the gospel to be effectively presented to the Waray.

Information Needed to Answer the Research Questions

For the development of a contextual theology, I needed to learn the Waray views about God, healing (especially the source), the spirit world, death, supernatural power and causation, and theology of the weather. I also needed to learn the cultural issues that impact and are impacted by Waray religious beliefs. Furthermore, I also needed to know what the Bible says about idolatry, God's providence, allegiance to God or idols, spirit possession and the supremacy of Jesus name, theology of blessing, Christology as it pertains to Christ's mediation and the doctrine of the baptism in the Holy Spirit. I also needed to learn the cultural issues that impact Waray religious beliefs. In order to understand the appeal of the gospel to the Waray, I needed to understand the history and development of Assemblies of God churches in this region and focus on what has been preached, taught and practiced to draw people to Christ. Specifically I needed to know how the lives of the Assemblies of God population have been changed as a result of the gospel.

Sources of Information

Books, theses, dissertations and other written materials on the Waray have provided a wealth of information for this study. From these sources I developed two questionnaires and one interview designed to provide the data necessary for answering the research questions.

The first questionnaire was administered by trained researchers to both a randomly selected sample of the General Population (hereinafter referred to as the GP) living in the *barangays,* which are small geopolitical units and a selected sample of members and adherents of Assemblies of God (hereinafter referred to as the AG) churches in the region. These population samples were determined through using standard procedures for behavioral sciences research. Twenty *barangays* and twenty-four Assemblies of God churches were selected. Chi-square analysis was used whenever possible to determine if the differences of opinion between the two sample populations were significant.

The AG respondents were further divided into members, adherents and pastors. To be a member of an Assemblies of God church, one has to be baptized in water. Adherents (or sympathizers as they are known in the Philippines) are those who have not yet been baptized and in some cases may not have yet received Christ, but are attending a Bible study, church services, or have in some way indicated an interest in the church.

A second questionnaire was administered only to Assemblies of God people by the same researchers immediately after the respondents had answered the questions to the first questionnaire. This questionnaire was designed to study how the gospel had impacted their lives and changed their worldview.

A third research instrument, an interview questionnaire guide known as *Questionnaire Regarding the History and Development of the*

Assemblies of God in the Leyte/Samar region, was an open ended interview with the pioneer pastors who led the way in planting the first Assemblies of God churches in the region.

This data was collected, analyzed in chapters five through ten and compared, along with the literature, to what the Bible teaches about each related theological issue. Specific contact points were made between what the Bible teaches and elements of the Waray belief system such as the reality of spiritual power, spiritual mediation, spirit possession, the deity of Christ and other Assemblies of God beliefs. I then evaluated how closely related the religious beliefs of the Waray are to the Bible and proposed ways to explain and demonstrate the gospel more clearly to them.

Scope and Limitations of This Study

This study attempted to understand the religious beliefs of the Waray people as they relate to their animistic practices. Specific themes included worldview and spirit world issues, folk Roman Catholic practices that are steeped in animism, supernatural power and issues related to nature. Biblical beliefs that are relevant to these subjects were studied to determine whether the Waray beliefs are similar and how biblical truth can be brought to bear on the lives of the Waray people.

The history of the Assemblies of God among the Waray was reviewed with specific attention given to what has been preached and practiced in evangelistic, church planting and discipleship efforts and how the people's lives were changed as a result.

While many issues concerning contextualization were covered, specific emphasis was given to contextual issues arising from Waray animistic practices because they encompass all areas of life. However, no claim is made here to an exhaustive effort at contextualization. The focus here is on the proclamation of the gospel message and to the initial follow-up process.

Before we can delve into the theological issues, however, we will look into the history of the Assemblies of God in the region. Along the way, we will pick up hints as to how the gospel has impacted and changes the lives of the members and adherents.

Chapter 1

HISTORY AND DEVELOPMENT OF THE ASSEMBLIES OF GOD IN THE LEYTE/SAMAR REGION

The history of the Assemblies of God among the Waray is a chronicle of the Lord's marvelous work and the dedication and sacrifice of many servants of God. The implications of this activity of God and the work of His servants must form the backdrop for any attempt to explore a contextual theology. To understand what God has done, my questionnaire on the history and development of the Assemblies of God was administered to twenty-seven pastors. This questionnaire was given both to the pastors whose churches were selected for the research as well as those who were identified as pioneers in the district. The answers to that questionnaire form the backbone for this chapter.

The Assemblies of God churches in the Leyte/Samar region are a part of the Philippine General Council of the Assemblies of God (PGCAG), with national headquarters in Valenzuela City, Metro Manila. The PGCAG is divided into geographical districts, each with it's own leadership. For the sake of simplicity, the Assemblies of God churches in the Leyte/Samar region will be referred to here as Assemblies of God, or AG. In the early days, the churches in the Leyte/Samar region fell under the Visayas Northern Mindanao District Council, known better by its acronym, VISNOMIN. They later separated and formed the Eastern Visayas District Council (EVDC). Two dominant people groups live in the region of the EVDC, the Waray and the Cebuanos. My focus here, however, is only on the Waray. The history can be divided into three time periods.

The First Period (1960-1972)

The only church planter among the Waray of this period, as far as I could determine, was Pedro Sumulat, who was a Waray. Sumulat and his family moved to Catbalogan, Western Samar, in 1960, after his graduation from Immanuel Bible Institute (now College) in Cebu City. There they pioneered Bethel Temple Assembly of God, the first Pentecostal church of any kind on the entire island.

Sumulat said that the Lord called him back to his own island while he was studying in Bible school. In his own words (2001):

> I was still in Bible school when the Lord directed me to start the work. I said 'Lord, where?' He said you've got to go back to Samar. I said 'well Lord, I think it was clear that a prophet has no honor in his own country.' The Lord made it so clear. [The] Lord said, 'are you after honor?'

In the end, the Sumulats obeyed the Lord and moved to Catbalogan, Western Samar, to begin the Assemblies of God work among the Waray.

Pioneering was hard work. According to Sumulat, the Holy Spirit told him that he would make him a stranger among his own people. Many of the people rejected them, thinking they were some kind of cult. Although Sumulat repeatedly stated that he had come to share the Good News about Jesus Christ in house to house visitation, his message seemed to fall on deaf ears. While this was disheartening, the Sumulats recognized that there was a lot of cultivation to do in pioneering work, and they persevered.

Two of the keys to the Sumulats' success in Catbalogan were birthed in his life while he was in Bible school. By his own confession, he was never a great student, but he thrived in being in the presence of God. On many occasions, classes had to be cancelled because of the moving of the Spirit in the chapel services. He testified that they would "wallow on the floor and speak in tongues." When he became president of a student-led organization within the school, there was a great moving of the Holy Spirit that did not cease right up to his graduation, growing "from fire to fire." Throughout the interview, he repeatedly emphasized the power of the Holy Spirit and, regarding his Bible school experience, preferred the experience of Pentecost over book learning.

The second key came from a classmate who, through his own example, challenged Sumulat to believe God for the impossible. Taking this to heart while pioneering in Catbalogan, they continued to reach out in spite of the difficulties. After a while they returned to some of the same people who initially rejected them and, for some unknown reason, they were received. Then they began to pray for the sick and many were healed. In two years, the church was established with a lot and a building.

Around 1966, the Sumulat family, which now included four children, felt it was time to make a change, motivated, at least in part, by their unstable financial situation. Apparently his wife was enrolled in college in Catbalogan at the time, studying to be a teacher. Leaving the youngest with her, he turned the church over to another pastor and moved to Tacloban City to pioneer another church.

After arriving in Tacloban, Sumulat secured a house to use as a church. A highlight of his ministry there was a month long evangelistic crusade. While he was putting up posters for the meetings around town, someone misunderstood what he was doing and wanted to shoot him. Thankfully, this was never carried out. On the opening night of the meetings, a thunderstorm threatened to ruin everything. In response, Sumulat said he lifted his hands to the Lord and commanded the rain to be diverted over the nearby mountains. After he prayed, the thunderstorm split in two, one part passing over the mountains to one side and the second over the sea. It never rained in the city.

The crusade itself was marked by a number of signs and wonders. In one instance, three women from a nearby town came, bringing a girl who was deaf and dumb because she was demon possessed. After preaching for about five minutes, he stopped and called the girl to the platform, announcing to the crowd that they were about to see a powerful demonstration of the power of the Lord. He prayed over her with simple, child-like faith, and she was instantly healed!

One day during the crusade, they were still praying for the sick when the time expired on their permit for the use of the crusade site. Seeing what was happening, the chief of police came up to Sumulat and told him not to worry as he was extending their time limit. Therefore, they kept on praying and many were healed. On the third day of the meeting, a childless couple came to him for prayer. He challenged them to believe that God would give them what they desired, prayed for them and was later informed that the woman became pregnant within a week after he had prayed.

Sadly, however, the fruit of the crusade was not conserved. Sumulat said that only a few came to the church. He did not say why this was so, although he said he failed to believe God for the impossible as he had done in Catbalogan. Roque Cagas (2001), the district superintendent of the region at that time, said that when the couple who had opened their home to the Sumulats moved to Manila, the church was closed. While this must have been disappointing to the Sumulat family, God was not finished with them. Neither was the denominational leadership, who sent them on to Guiuan, Eastern Samar, to begin the Assemblies of God work there.

The Sumulats' ministry in Guiuan would be their longest in terms of years, the most challenging and the most fruitful. Nowadays one can travel by road from Tacloban City to Guiuan in a matter of hours. In 1969, however, the fastest way was by boat. They arrived at the pier in Guiuan about four o'clock in the morning and, in what would be a portent of things to come, no one would take them in or rent a house to them because they were not Catholic. By now the family had grown to five children so this quickly became a serious issue. They ended up staying right on the pier for four days. While they did manage to find some shelter in a shed there, the roof leaked. Even trying to fix the leak with a blanket didn't help as rain came through anyway. Sumulat admits that he made the same mistake here that he made in Tacloban in not believing God for the impossible.

After repenting of his lack of faith, he began to fast and pray. Then he ran into a retired policeman. The officer mentioned that there was a cottage for rent in an abandoned cemetery near the sea, but that no one wanted it because it was haunted. Sumulat responded: "I think he [the demon possessing the house] will not be able to withstand against the gospel's power. The Lord commanded us to preach the gospel and it is our business in coming. For I know the gospel is the power of God unto salvation..." They moved in and there were no further problems with demons in the house.

From the beginning, however, the local priest and nuns opposed the Sumulats and told people not to accept them. Only children came at first. They became discouraged but kept working and praying.

One day he prayed for a sick man and the man was healed. Revival broke out. Then one night, many sick people came for prayer and God healed them. By this time, however, then President Ferdinand Marcos had declared martial law, meaning that no one could be out on the streets after a certain hour. The meeting that night ran until about midnight so the people would have to violate martial law to get home. God gave Sumulat favor with the police, however, and they took the people home in their patrol car!

When revival broke out, persecution intensified. The priest became angry, recognizing that if he did not do something, his people would be going over to the Assembly of God church. In the end, the priest was able to have twenty-one families jailed on unspecified charges. Sumulat was required to post an enormous sum for bail. By this time, the church had secured property and another missions organization had constructed a building. When he went to the prison to get the people, the warden said he had noted the joy of the Lord in the hearts of the people. While in prison, the people had conducted services day and night. The persecution, however, did not end. New charges were filed against Sumulat personally and the case ended up in the national Supreme Court. This took a long time to resolve and he was not exonerated until 1990, the Court agreeing that he had been abused. When asked how he dealt with all of this, he just said that the Lord told him just to rejoice and preach Christ.

The most tragic incident of persecution came while he was away from his family. For a number of years Sumulat served as a presbyter, an overseer for the Assemblies of God churches in Leyte and Samar. One time, while he was in Tacloban fulfilling his responsibilities, he received a telegram from his wife saying that their youngest son had become ill and was hospitalized. While there, he was given too much medication and died. To this day, while he has never been able to prove it, Sumulat believes that his boy was murdered by the order of the Catholic priest. While he was understandably angry and considered filing charges, the Lord instructed him not to do so, but to love his enemies instead.

One of his persistent persecutors was a young woman named Luz Pascua, who thought he was insane. In time, however, Luz opened her heart to the Lord and was saved. After studying at Zion Bible Institute, she began pastoring another Assemblies of God church right there in Guiuan and, according to Sumulat, the work flourished.

The Sumulats illustrate the fact that the first period was characterized by hardships and hope that the seed of the gospel would germinate and grow. As the Sumulats and others planted the seed, God confirmed his word through signs and wonders. The seed grew. When I interviewed him many years later, Sumulat rejoiced at the number of Assemblies of God churches that have sprung up on Samar since 1960.

The Second Period (1972-1988)

By 1972, there were about six Assemblies of God churches in the Leyte/Samar region. As far as I can verify, the two churches pioneered by Sumulat in Catbalogan and Guiuan were the only existing churches among the Waray at that time.

This began to change when a man named Nazario Sadorra, a layman who owned property in Western Samar, felt a burden to train Waray pastors to reach their own people (Eguia 1989:18, 21-22). He shared this vision with superintendent Cagas, who agreed on the need for a Bible school in the region. In 1972, Zion Bible Institute (ZBI) was born in Catbalogan, Eastern Samar, with ten students and a pastor, Levi Montes, as founding president.

Montes said that the goal of reaching the Waray for Christ was to be achieved by church planting, using Bible School students as pioneer workers. This methodology not only provided hands-on training for the students, but also served to evangelize the nearby communities. The students were sent out into the surrounding communities on the weekends to plant churches, with the school providing fare and food. Eleven churches were planted while Zion was in Samar and more have been planted since it's move to Leyte.

Nena Ibañez (2001), the ZBI president at the time of my research, stated that church planting remains at the heart of the school's vision, as well as providing pastors and church workers for established churches. In the course of conducting these interviews, a number of pastors reiterated these goals, suggesting that the school has been successful in communicating and executing its vision. While the goal may have been to train the Waray for ministry, God had also called many Cebuanos to plant churches among the Waray. Of the twenty-four churches that we visited in the course of this research, eight were pastored by Cebuanos.

Miriam Cruiz (2001), a teacher at the school since 1976, also noted that many other churches were opened but did not survive because the workers assigned to them did not continue once they finished Bible school. The reasons given for not continuing were lack of finances and the youth and immaturity of the workers (graduates may have been as young as 19-20 years old). Also, the attitude in some quarters of the Assemblies of God that bi-vocational ministry is not appropriate for a pastor may have contributed to the problem.

For the first nine years, ZBI was located in Western Samar. According to Montes, life was hard there because of lack of funds. Cagas was able to get some support for the school from a charitable foundation in Cebu for a couple of years, but that, too, eventually dried up. Joey Eguia (1989:19), a faculty member in the 1980s, notes that one of the reasons that things were financially difficult was because the students were not required to pay tuition. The results were both negative and positive—low pay for the faculty and not much food for the students, but enrollment was high. Despite hard times, the leadership and faculty of the school remained committed to the task. The students caught fish to eat and Sadorra donated a piece of land which the students farmed for awhile but were later stopped because of civil unrest. Because the land was in a rural area far from the highway, it was not suitable for residence.

Originally, at the church's invitation, dormitories and classrooms were built on the campus of Bethel Temple, the church in Catbalogan pioneered by Sumulat. In 1974, they were finally able to buy land about two kilometers north of Bethel Temple, providing more space for the growing student body. An old piggery on the property was converted into dorms and classroom space. Part of this land was also used for farming. In a sense, then, the students did help pay for their education by farming the land, fishing, or doing chores around the school.

Because the pay for the faculty was low and, at times, non-existent, no one was able to teach fulltime. This meant that the faculty, normally made up of pastors, had to keep pastoring in order to have an income. The weakness of this type of an arrangement is that it can lead to lack of on-campus leadership since the teachers had to leave after class to attend to other responsibilities. Zion's solution to this issue, at least at its current campus, has been to provide housing for at least some of the faculty and administration right on the school grounds. Another weakness of the part-time faculty situation is that, because they need to tend to other responsibilities, they do not have the time or financial resources for theological reflection and deeper study that would enhance their teaching.

But there are also some distinct advantages. People who have to pastor as well as teach are much more likely to be in touch with the needs of the local church than full-time faculty members who may fall prey to the temptation of academic isolation. Another advantage is that because the faculty are also pastoring, they can take students to their church's outstations on the weekends and give them practical mentoring and training. In these situations, good relationships can be built between the faculty and student body on several different levels and may lead to some meaningful, lifelong friendships.

In 1978 an independent missionary named Carl Alemania assumed the presidency of the school. From then on, students were required to pay tuition (Eguia 1989: 20). Because of this requirement and the fact that other free Bible schools were operating in the region, student enrollment dropped. ZBI's leadership, however, remained true to the vision. In 1977, new Assemblies of God missionaries, Jim and Betty Curtis, moved into the area and also served at the school. Curtis had first received a burden for this region when he came ashore at Palo, Leyte, in the liberation of the Philippines in World War II.

In 1980, Curtis, then serving as president of the school, invited missionary-evangelist Mayme Williams to the campus. While she was there, she got a burden for the school and saw that some changes would benefit Zion. She encouraged them to move to a better location, saying that there was no room for further development where they were. Eguia (1989:20) adds that the poor living conditions were also part of her motivation for recommending change and also noted that another location would be more strategic for evangelism and church planting. Taking action on her burden, she raised the necessary funds. In 1981, the Bible school moved to its present location in Palo, Leyte, just outside of Tacloban City, along the highway that leads to much of the rest of the island. While the property was cheap, some of the land was swampy and needed to be filled in with dirt. Temporary classrooms and dormitories were then constructed along with a temporary nipa wood administration building. Classes began in July of 1981, only a few weeks behind the projected starting date.

Eguia (1989:21) notes that God continued to bless the school. In time, the temporary buildings were replaced by more permanent ones, thanks mainly to William's continued fundraising efforts. In the mid-eighties, the faculty was also augmented by several Filipino teachers with master's degrees, some of them native to the area. New missionaries Mark and Fredda Alston and Margaret Pashley also joined the school during this time.

By 1989, there were more than seventy-five alumni of ZBI. While some had left the area or joined other organizations, the vast majority remained in the region and identified themselves with the Assemblies of God (Eguia 1989:22). Some were involved in church planting and others in pastoring existing churches, furthering the vision of reaching the Waray for Christ.

In addition to their responsibilities at Zion, Jim and Betty Curtis were involved in a variety of other ministries. These ministries included constructing six church buildings and helping to found Teen Challenge, a coffee house ministry street people. While the Teen Challenge did not succeed in the long term, the people who were reached through this ministry helped to form a new church, Living Word Fellowship in Tacloban City, pioneered by Levi Montes.

From 1979-1984, Jim Curtis also directed a boat ministry. Pump boats were built and pastors were trained as boat captains who held evangelistic crusades on the smaller islands in the Leyte/Samar region and planted a number of churches. Eguia (1989:16) reports that by 1989, nine boats were operational under the leadership of short term missionary Jack Hindman, a relative of Curtis, and five churches had been planted on the smaller islands in the Leyte/Samar region. Probably because of the high maintenance costs, the boat ministry ceased sometime after the Curtises moved to Manila in 1984.

The Alstons arrived in December, 1986, with Dorothy, their daughter. While serving in various capacities at the Bible school, including president for a time, they also focused on church planting.

In the late 90's Mark Alston, feeling that the Bible school was not graduating students fast enough to reach the lost and plant new churches, got a burden for a short-term training program to train lay people to plant cell churches. In order to provide this training, construction was completed on the Net Center near Borongan, Eastern Samar, in a beautiful spot beside the sea in 2001. Before the vision could be implemented the Alstons, unfortunately, needed to take a medical furlough in the States because of Fredda's health. Local churches have, thankfully, been able to make some use of the building for their activities.

When Margaret Pashley arrived in 1988, she spent her first few months studying the Waray language (Eguia 1989:17) and then began serving at ZBI as a faculty member, outreach director, and succeeded Alston as president. Fellow faculty member Miriam Cruiz notes that Pashley, like the ZBI presidents before her, had a vision for sending out Pentecostal church planters. She worked with students and new graduates in church planting and particularly used a church plant in Palo to train students in outreach activities before handing it over to a national pastor. For several years Pashley worked with two former students, Vicky Vidas and Gil Ballon. In 1996 and 1997 they surveyed the three provinces of Samar to ascertain the extent of Christian witness in the towns, and showed the Jesus Film. Pashley's final church plant was in year 2000 at Quinapondon, Eastern Samar, where Vidas accepted the challenge to pastor the work.

In addition to her other responsibilities, in 1997, Pashley, seeing the continual struggle of pastors to support their families, began a sponsorship program for pastor's kids. Individual sponsors from Australia were recruited and a cash amount given to the pastors to assist in providing for the needs of their children, greatly relieving the financial stress on the families. As of 2001, 190 children were being sponsored. Feeling a burden to begin ministry to street children, many of whom were substance abusers, she formed a foundation and, with a faithful team of volunteers, began reaching out to people in 2001. They secured temporary rented housing in 2002; by 2004 they purchased land, and the team and children moved into three houses by January 2005. By 2012 a village of ten homes, school, skills training and other facilities existed to care for needy children, giving them a hope and a future.

However, this project put her at odds with her mission and she found it necessary to resign her AG missionary appointment, although she remained in contact with the local Assemblies of God churches. But in August, 2012, she accepted an offer to reconnect with her mission as an associate field worker.

The relationship between the missionaries and the national church is not easily evaluated. While they each had their own separate leadership, they both aimed toward the same goal of establishing the work of God among the Waray. The missionaries perception of their relationship with the national church was difficult to ascertain as only Mark Alston commented on the issue:

> When we first went to work with Waraywarays I was extremely concerned about indigeniety. The four stages of mission being pioneer, paternalism, partnership and

participation... Paternalism was the dominant stage when we arrived as rookie missionaries and I overreacted, not wanting to perpetuate paternalism. My relationship with the national leaders has been good but not what it could have been if I had nurtured partnership principles properly. I should have consulted more with the national leadership on all aspects of my plans even to the point of allowing them to veto some of my plans. They know so much more of the 'ground' than I will ever know. Today I plan to run everything I do first via the district leadership and get their input and listen to their concerns about my projects. Before I did not partner but fell into a more paternalistic mode due to the reality that existed at the time. Today the district leadership considers me 'their' Leyte/Samar missionary, which I consider to the greatest honor that I could ever attain as an American missionary.

Paternalism, a stage of mission where the missionary is in charge of the development of the church, was not Alston's model, but he struggled to reach the ideal as do many missionaries.

In summarizing the work of the Assemblies of God during the 70s and 80s, more than twenty churches were planted, mostly under the auspices of the Bible school. Therefore, this time period can be characterized as a period of modest but healthy growth for the AG in the Leyte/Samar region. With a vision for reaching the region for Christ comes the two-fold challenge of raising up leadership and funding new works. While these challenges are never ending, Zion has answered the demand for leadership training for church planting and pastoral ministry. With the growth, however, came more challenges, but also more opportunities.

The Third Period (From 1988 Onward)

When ZBI was started in 1972, there were only about six churches and a handful of pastors in the region. By 1988, the number of churches had grown to around thirty churches. There were also credentialed ministers.

More churches and pastors, however, increase the need for administrative and pastoral care. Because of the increased demand, some of the local leaders began to feel that VISNOMIN had grown too large and that its district office in Cebu City was too far away to provide the oversight and care needed. The difficulties associated with pastoral care over a large territory were compounded by the lack of telephone service at the time and the lack of personal vehicles. Leaders especially struggled with travel to rural areas where transportation was less dependable. But part of the felt need for clear pastoral leadership may have also been cultural. Even though this is changing with the advent of cell phones and increased mass communications, the Waray, like most Filipinos, are a people who prefer personal contact. Their indirect personal communication style demands that non-verbal signs, such as facial expressions and body language, be read face-to-face. This may have been the underlying reason why they felt that they needed to bring the district leadership closer to home.

As early as 1984, movement began towards creating a separate district. A petition was filed with the General Council to separate from VISNOMIN which was not acted upon until 1988 (Eguia 1989:6). In the process, however, a problem developed. The island of Leyte is divided into two provinces, Northern Leyte and Southern Leyte. The province of Northern Leyte is mostly Waray, but Southern Leyte is largely Cebuano. The VISNOMIN district, like the others in the Assemblies of God, was divided into sections along geographical lines. The churches in Northern Leyte were part of the Upper Leyte Section and the churches in Southern Leyte comprised the Lower Leyte section. According to Eguia (1989:8), Levi Montes, the guiding spirit behind the new district, said that the leadership of both sections were aware of the plans and philosophy of forming a new district. The leaders of Lower Leyte, however, told Eguia that no formal invitation was ever extended to them to join the new district. Eguia may be correct in saying that the initiators of the new district were probably overly confident that the Southern section would join the others.

This does not mean that the Lower Leyte Section was unaware of what was happening. The lack of a formal invitation may or may not have been the real issue behind their resistance to the prospect of the new district. The Waray, as well as other Filipinos tend to be loyal to individual leaders, not to organizations. Personal loyalty to the VISNOMIN district superintendent, Roque Cagas, a Cebuano, appears to have played a strong role in the Lower Leyte section's reluctance to join the new district, as Eguia (1989:9) notes that they had a strong affinity to him. In the end, the churches of Lower Leyte did not support the move to separate from VISNOMIN.

While the refusal of lower Leyte to join was a blow and may have held up the process, in the end, the pastors of upper Leyte and Samar succeeded in their quest to form a new district. In 1988, probably April, the General Council of the Assemblies of God recognized the new district, originally called the Leyte-Samar district, and known today as the Eastern Visayas District Council. In October of that same year, the first district convention was held and Montes was elected as the first superintendent. Mernilo Illuminado Jr. (2001) noted that the separation from VISNOMIN was amicable.

The financial situation was not good at first but improved over time. Cruz Lapura (2001), states that adequately supporting pastors, especially in pioneer works, is still a major challenge. In commenting on church planting, Ulpie Cabael (2001) points out that the most persistent problems for pioneering pastors are hunger, temptation, and lack of progress in the work. In light of these realities, pastoral care from district and sectional leaders is imperative in order to provide encouragement, help in dealing with temptation and, as much as possible, provide financial support.

Another persistent challenge has been persecution. While there is no government sanctioned persecution of Christians and the level of persecution related by Pedro Sumulat may be a bit extreme, persecution at a local level from the Catholic church was common. The strongest persecution, however, is normally within families. Eguia (1989:11) said that there was a general openness among students to the gospel through the witness of Agape Christian Fellowship, an Assemblies of God college ministry. However, this openness was repressed by the older generation in the home who clung to the old ways.

Another challenge has been the New People's Army (NPA), a communist guerilla movement that has terrorized parts of the nation for decades. While the strength of this movement tends to ebb and flow depending on the national and world political situation, it has always had a presence in the Leyte/Samar region, particularly Samar. The insurgents, in many cases armed, have been known to impose a "revolutionary tax" on local businesses, rob people on the highways and live off the local people, causing general havoc. One of the root causes that gives rise to the communist ideals of the NPA is poverty. The prevalence of witchcraft and sorcery also casts a pall of darkness over the region and impoverishes the people. In spite of all of these challenges, however, the work of the Assemblies of God continues.

Between the formation of the new district in 1988 and the time of my field research in 2001 more than fifty additional new churches were planted. The Spirit of God is at work and there is much cause for rejoicing. God is answering the prayers of those hardy pioneers who planted the seed, watered it and trusted God to make it grow. How the church grew is a valid question and to that story we now turn.

Chapter 2

METHODS, MESSAGE, AND MIRACLES

The story of how the Assemblies of God grew in the Leyte/Samar region is a study in both contextualized church planting methodology and Pentecostal practice. This practice embraces the concept that miracles are indispensable to announcing the arrival of God's Kingdom (Matthew 10:7-8). In this section, the methods and message of the pastors interviewed, as well as the impact of miracles in the lives of the people, will be discussed. But before turning to the research results, two major region-wide evangelistic methods will be considered.

The AG as a whole expects that churches will mother new churches in their own neighboring communities. A pastor or members may feel a burden for another part of their area that is beyond the reach of their church or members living at a distance from the church may request that a church be opened in their area.

In these situations, the normal procedure is to go door to door and invite people to a home Bible study. If a crusade can be held, the fruit of the crusade is normally gathered into these studies as well. In the case of a crusade, about three months is needed to weed out those who are not serious about following the Lord. During this time the pastor or his appointed worker will teach on the basics of the Christian faith. In time, new believers are baptized and a new church is born.

Another method is radio ministry. Pastor Rening Castino (2001) relates that those involved in radio ministry would survey the people listening to the radio programs and then go to the location of the listeners to conduct radio rallies in person. She also related that they encouraged local pastors to follow up on people, who would invite them to church or would send a worker to conduct home Bible studies. They also counseled people over the airwaves and by mail which helped to build relationships. Cruz Lapura, who worked with Castino in this effort, states that many people have come to know the Lord and their lives have been changed through this ministry and many churches have been planted in the *barangays*. Many have also been healed when someone prayed for them over the radio, including a man who had been paralyzed.

These programs are sponsored by the Asia Pacific Media Ministries (APMM), an Asia Pacific wide media effort of the Assemblies of God that is based in Manila. Bill Snider, the director of APMM, states that many churches have been planted by this method in Samar. The radio ministry among the Waray must be judged as a phenomenal success.

The advantage of using radio is that the gospel can be shared over a much wider geographical area and people can listen in the privacy of their own homes. Since radio is impersonal, the local radio rallies and the follow-up by the local pastors provide the necessary personal touch. The one drawback of radio ministry may be the cost of producing radio programs which is difficult for many churches to shoulder. However, this can be overcome if the churches will band together and give sacrificially.

In looking at the substantial growth that took place in the 90s, it seems fair to suggest that the initiative for church planting has passed from the Bible school to the local churches themselves. Since the Bible school can only send its students to the areas surrounding the school on the weekends, the churches need to carry the burden of church planting if the whole region is to be reached.

The Evangelistic Methods Used

The pastors interviewed were asked what methods they used to reach the Waray and which methods were successful and which were not. Many of these are incorporated in their church planting efforts.

TABLE 2.1
Evangelism Methods

Successful	Unsuccessful	Method
24	3	House to house/personal evangelism
16	9	Have evangelistic crusade/film showing/street meeting
9	2	Home Bible studies, finding contacts
6	2	Feeding Programs

House to house evangelism was by far the most popular evangelism method. Social contact and interpersonal relationships are important to the Waray. Several pastors explained why personal evangelism done this way is important to their strategy. Joseline Squadra (2001) noted that "Filipinos have lots of friends and Waray people like to be visited." Johnny Opena (2001) said that house to house evangelism works because attention can be given to individuals, making them feel special. One can more easily know the needs of people with this kind of evangelism.

Maricel Gacoscosim (2001), noting advantages of the high unemployment rate, gives some details of the how and why of this strategy:

> When they don't work, you can go in and share the gospel undisturbed and offer your friendship to them and they become more and more open to sharing their needs. They feel important when people take time to come see them, especially if they become sick. They become open to sharing their burdens. First friendship. They don't need a direct sharing of the gospel at first. If you share directly from the beginning they will put up a wall.

The key, according to Gacoscosim and some of the other pastors interviewed, is to build relationships before sharing the gospel and confronting people with their sin. Good, long term, relationships are a bridge over which the gospel can cross. One of the reasons that people might put up walls if there is no relationship is that the true gospel is so contrary to what the people have been taught all their lives.

Naomi Besere (2001) says that they concentrate on homes where someone requests prayer for healing. This method almost guarantees gaining entrance to the home and finding a receptive audience. Nestor (2001) agrees that house to house visitation is successful because of the relationship factor, allowing the workers to pray for people's needs specifically. Because house to house evangelism has been highly successful, Alston sees this as a key component in church planting. House visitation can also be combined with other forms of evangelism, such as crusades.

Two pastors found house to house visitation to be unsuccessful. One stated that:

> House to house visitation with a big Bible in your hand, for them it's another religion, and people are afraid of the word born again because in their thinking, they will not depart from their old faith and becoming born again in another group could change their religion [sic].

In this case the methodology was flawed. The first might have found it more successful had she taken a more subtle approach with a smaller Bible in her purse. Lapura said that their workers administered a questionnaire asking such questions as: what church do you attend? Are you attending Sunday School? However, he confessed that this method wasn't all that effective and few were won. A questionnaire that is used to sincerely determine religious preferences is fine, but if the motive here was to use it to get into someone's home to then share the gospel, another methodology should have been used.

Sixteen reported that some kind of evangelistic crusade was effective. Because of the average Waray's reluctance to enter a non-Catholic church, most of these outreaches are done outside in a basketball court or plaza. Probably the most popular type of evangelistic crusade involves showing an evangelistic Christian film, preferably in Tagalog or Waray. The film itself is intended to draw the crowd and can also help to convey the message of salvation.

In my own experience, when films are used the best strategy is to stop the film at a high drama point to prevent the crowd from going home and present our program which normally involves music, occasionally testimonies and preaching an evangelistic message with an altar call. Afterwards, we finish the film. The greatest advantage to this type of ministry is that it provides new contacts for the church which can really give a boost to a new church plant.

Open-air crusades also present excellent opportunities for the power of God to be revealed to unbelievers, especially in healing. A disadvantage is that, if one compares the number of names on the decision cards to those who actually follow Christ when the follow-up is completed, the percentage is usually low. The success or failure of such an event has little to do with the quality of the program or preaching, but has everything to do with the genuine level of interest and follow-up.

Nine also reported home Bible studies to be effective. There are many advantages to this method. Even the poorest churches in the barrios can sponsor these Bible studies, the only cost being the transportation of the pastor or worker conducting the Bible study. Another is that a home is a place where people feel comfortable to attend and ask whatever questions might be on their hearts. Two pastors reported that home Bible studies did not work for them. One pastor said that he mobilized members but failed to train them.

Another challenge to this method is that, unless the new believers are incorporated in the regular church worship services, they may not become involved in the body life of the church. Perhaps this is why Gabato (2001) recommends that Bible studies "be balanced with cell groups where they learn worship and singing and the Holy Spirit can work in them." Cell groups, while not apparently common among the Waray, may provide an effective bridge to bring people from home Bible studies into the corporate life of the church. Planting house churches, as my wife and I are currently encouraging in the Bicol region, are also effective in bringing people to greater maturity and involvement in the Body of Christ.

In looking at the above mentioned methods, one can easily see that they work well and are usually used best in combination with one another. For example, workers can be sent out to invite people to a film showing crusade, usually handing out gospel literature to people as they go along. Those who receive Christ in the crusade are normally gathered first into home Bible studies and, in time, hopefully into the corporate life of the church. Many of these kinds of Bible studies also form the foundation of new churches.

A good example of using a variety of methods in combination is a church plant done by Margaret Pashley when she co-pioneered a church in Quinapondan, Eastern Samar. She states that they did a month of evangelistic activities which included concerts, gospel films, Bible studies, sports and serving snacks to the town officials and the elderly—which she says helped to break down barriers of suspicion. After this month of activities, she returned weekly to do follow-up. The church continues to do well today under Filipino leadership.

Six pastors also found feeding programs to be effective. Squadra (2001) also adds that feeding programs are a wonderful asset to reaching people through meeting their physical needs. This is a tangible expression of the love of God. The Childcare Community Ministries of the Philippines is a good example. This national child feeding program, sponsored by the Assemblies of God USA, has provided some feeding stations among the Waray. Their program consisted of providing a noon meal in an Assemblies of God church to twenty children who are selected on the basis of physical need. A nurse oversees the program, weighs the children weekly and teaches nutrition and basic sanitation to their mothers. The pastor of the church teaches a Bible study where at least one of the parents of each child was required to attend. The vast majority of these parents receive Christ and about seventy percent remain true to the faith. Two respondents, however, said that feeding programs were not effective. Pashley said they were not helpful because those who received help expected to continue to receive help from the churches. Another disadvantage is that feeding programs are expensive and therefore not reproducible by most local churches. If there are no funds from the outside, such programs cannot normally be sustained.

Some pastors found other methods effective such as tract distribution, which is best done in combination with another form of outreach. In other cases, the pastors saw an opportunity to do something that would help them build relationships in the community which, in time, might open doors for witness. Examples would be teaching at a secular university, giving piano lessons and even circumcising children.

Lest one be tempted to think that successful evangelism, in the final analysis, rests on correct methodology, Lapura (2001) notes:

> Then it is the Holy Spirit who convicts them [people], and they accept the Lord. I can't say I really have a successful method. Unlike other ministers who have a method that is successful, I don't have that kind. If people are converted, then, they have to come to Jesus Christ, and I believe that is the work of the Holy Spirit.

Methods are important but are worthless unless the Holy Spirit moves.

Prayer is necessary to the moving of the Holy Spirit. Ranon (2001) expresses this thought beautifully:

You need also to pray in order to be effective. Prayer is the bridge of evangelism. Spiritual warfare is important because of spiritual bondage. So prayer evangelism is an important strategy because the Waray-Waray are bound by witchcraft and idolatry.

For evangelism to be successful, the Holy Spirit must guide and direct the pastors and churches, through prayer, to methods that should be employed and when.

The Message: Subjects Taught or Recommended

Each respondent was asked to answer two questions regarding what should be taught in home Bible studies or in a new church planting effort. The first was, "In your opinion, what Bible teachings were the most effective in bringing people to Christ?" The second was "If I were going to plant a church among the Waray, what Bible subjects do you recommend that I teach or preach on in evangelistic outreaches and discipleship Bible studies?"

Because the situation of home Bible studies and a church planting effort are so similar and related many of the answers were redundant. For example, many of the pastors who said they teach salvation in their home Bible studies also said that they would recommend doing so in a new church planting situation. Thus, in order to reduce the redundancy in reporting the results of the questionnaire, the answers to the two questions are combined into one table below.

TABLE 2.2
Subjects Taught or Recommended

Number who teach this in home Bible Studies	Number who recommend teaching this in a church plant	Subjects Taught
20	14	Salvation/born again experience
6	5	Love of God
6	3	Eschatology
6	3	Repentance/change/forgiveness
6	2	True faith
5	1	Idolatry
4	8	Healing (1: healing, sickness and sin).
3	3	The Holy Spirit
3	4	Assurance of salvation
3	0	Will of God
3	9	Christian growth

Lapura explains that salvation is taught in these Bible studies because people do not understand the nature of salvation. This would include teaching on the basic doctrine of salvation, as well as telling people what they must do in order to be saved. This is even true when people receive Christ at an evangelistic rally or crusade as many really do not understand what has happened to them.

The challenge to bringing people to salvation is formidable. Cabael states that "the Waray already know they are sinners, and they will easily accept Christ. But the problem is it is hard for them to come to the church because they will always think you are bringing them to another kind of religion." He goes on to say that they

> Will always 'receive' Christ, but they are afraid of what their people will say. They are afraid of persecution from relatives, neighbors, and friends. So you must teach them about trials and criticism. If you take away the criticism and trials, they will all 'come to Christ.' There is a process of Bible study for them to fully comprehend the Christian life.

The love of God (or Christ) is also a popular issue because it is the basis for our salvation (cf. John 3:16) and because the people need to know that God loves them. A number of the pastors teach or recommended teaching eschatology, the doctrine of last things. Lemuel Matiga explains that he teaches this to let people know that one can have hope in God for the future. Animistic practices are focused on the present and Catholicism teaches purgatory, so preaching hope in Christ is attractive to the Waray. Gabato adds that she preaches the rapture, heaven, hell fire and the coming judgment, giving biblical credibility to the idea that there are consequences for sin and blessings for righteousness, concepts already present in Catholicism.

While only a few mentioned that they preach repentance, probably many more do so under the subject of salvation. True repentance, meaning to forsake sin and turn to righteousness, is an important subject in a Catholic context because Catholicism stresses penance, but not change. Regarding forgiveness, it is not clear whether they are referring to receiving forgiveness from God which would be a major component in teaching salvation or whether they are teaching that one can and must forgive others, an important subject among the revenge oriented Waray.

Regarding faith, most pastors here likely mean that they teach on how to have faith in God. In at least two instances, however, it meant in the sense of contending for the faith, i.e. apologetics. Gacoscosim (2001) holds that "there are many false beliefs here in Leyte and

Samar." Anyone who has spent time in the region would be hard pressed to disagree. Castino (2001) adds that the true faith must be contended for because the beliefs of the average Waray are not correct.

Regarding idolatry, most of the pastors with whom we spoke about this agreed that it was best not to deal with the issue right away. After a few months of Bible studies, the people are much more prepared to deal with these issues and the pastors have had the opportunity to establish a good relationship with them. With time, patience and good teaching, the people will realize for themselves that the saints cannot help them.

Four pastors also said they teach on healing, eight pastors recommending that other church planters do the same. A critical issue is where healing comes from since many believe it can come from God, the Virgin Mary or a host of other saints. One of the pastors, noting the reality of sickness of the heart as well as sickness of the body, also teaches healing both from sickness and sin.

Since spiritual power is at the root of idolatry, God's real power is needed in order to see people set free from idolatry. Primo Abayan (2001), a former idolater, uses himself as a example of what God can do in a person's life and why idolatry is wrong. Castino (2001) deals with idolatry by giving people a Bible so that they can find out what the Bible says about the issue and then answers questions about why there are no images in Assemblies of God churches. This gives her an opportunity to teach about the evils of idolatry. She adds that before they can become members of the church, they have to prove that they are no longer worshiping idols or wearing amulets.

It is rather surprising that so few mentioned teaching on the person and work of the Holy Spirit, as this is a cardinal Pentecostal doctrine. At least one of these pastors specifically mentioned teaching on the baptism in the Holy Spirit. Gabato (2001) said that she teaches the Holy Spirit's power to change lives, delivering people from the many vices in their community.

Assurance of salvation is an important teaching in the discipleship process. But care must be taken to teaching this only to those who have given solid evidence of true conversion, as there is always the danger of giving someone false assurance of salvation when there has been no real repentance.

Three pastors mentioned that they teach people how to know the will of God. This would include discovering God's plan for one's life as well as learning how to hear the voice of God and live in obedience to God's word. Sumodlayon (2001) teaches why God created men, what God's purpose is with man and the reasons for service to God.

In the Christian growth category, which includes sanctification and giving tithes and offerings, the overwhelming number of pastors who teach these subjects suggested they be taught when planting a church. Only three said that they should be taught initially in discipleship Bible studies. This may be because home Bible studies may have a lot of new believers or even unbelievers attending so other subjects, such as the nature of salvation, may need to be taught first.

Some teach various spiritual disciplines. One mentioned Bible study and meditation. A couple mentioned prayer. Gabato (2001) sees this as a wonderful opportunity to teach people to pray only to God and not to the saints. Spiritual warfare could also be placed under this category. Opena (2001) holds that even new believers must "know that there are two kingdoms at war with one another. If they don't, they won't get serious about the Lord." In comparison to the number of pastors interviewed, twenty-seven, the number of those who say that they teach spiritual disciplines is small. While there may well be others who also teach these things but didn't think to mention them, this issue may need to be addressed.

Others indicated teaching about water baptism or about the nature of God—which is important in dealing with idolatry. While formal Catholicism does not hold to the deity of Mary, Gabato (2001) says that many of the folk Catholics in her town believe in the deity of Mary and of St. Francis of Assissi, the patron saint of her town. Many other subjects are also taught or recommended including a biblical response to witchcraft—which will be dealt with extensively in chapters six through ten.

In looking over the list in Table 2.2, some general assessments are in order. First, since none of the pastors were given the questions in advance, all of their responses were extemporaneous. Many of them also were not particularly articulate in explaining what they teach. Therefore, it would seem likely that many of the subjects listed are probably taught more often than some of the numbers indicate. However, analysis here must be done based on the data at hand. Believers must understand the nature of sin and salvation in following Christ. They also need to teach about true faith, the love of God and eschatology, issues that can be well applied to the Waray social context.

Several additional areas of teaching, however, could strengthen the discipleship of the churches. First, as mentioned earlier, teaching is needed on the baptism of the Holy Spirit. The Bible not only teaches about the power of the written Word to change people's lives, it also reveals that God also displays his power through miracles. Second, also mentioned earlier, is the need to encourage new believers in spiritual disciplines for their growth. More attention could be given to teaching on the character of God the Father, which will help combat idolatry. A biblical perspective on family issues could help deal with domestic problems among the Waray.

The Role of Miracles

Each pastor was asked if miracles have been important in their ministry in bringing the Waray to Christ and if so, what kind? Twenty of the pastors said that healings were effective in bringing people to Christ. Nine also said that this was true of delivering people from demons and one added that deliverance from witchcraft also brought people to Christ.

Most of the pastors would agree with Illuminado (2001) that healings attract people to Christ. Ranon (2001) says that without miracles, the Waray won't believe. Healing and deliverance are what they need and that's what he gives them. He also related a story where a crippled man was healed and came to Christ because he saw that Christ was more powerful than the sorcerer. Cabael reported praying for a sick woman who testified that she was healed. She then began attending church and became more committed to Christ. Sumodlayon (2001) had a similar experience when two people were healed at a crusade in Catbalogan, Western Samar. Church members visited them and shared salvation; they received Christ and came to the church. The healing opened the door to sharing the Word of God. Gacoscosim (2001), however, first leads people in prayer for salvation before praying for their healing.

Healings not only impact those who are healed, they also impact others in the community. Gacoscosim notes that some people receive Christ when they see that other people are healed. Tordillos (2001) also testifies that other people receive Christ when they see God's healing power at work in the lives of their friends and relatives, as well as seeing their transformed lives. On the other hand, Primo Abayan (2001) says that many trusted Christ first, then were healed.

Some pastors, like Castino (2001), use opportunities to pray for the sick as a time to challenge the people's world view assumptions. When she goes to make house calls, she says that sometimes the people are wearing amulets on their bodies, which were placed there by witchdoctors. She then tells people that God will heal them and that the amulets are not necessary.

But not all who are healed accept the Lord. Ibañez, while stressing healing, notes that some follow the Lord after they have been healed, but some don't. Lemuel Matiga (2001) has also noted this phenomenon. But why is this so? It seems that if one was healed, one would surely want to follow the Lord. But because the Waray are so open to the supernatural, they are not always awed by it when it happens. Also, to the Waray way of thinking, the goal of someone requesting prayer when sick is the same as going to the witchdoctor to get healed. They are not nearly as concerned with who heals them as they are with getting healed.

For this reason, every opportunity must be taken soon after the healing to teach them the truth about God. When God has healed someone through the ministry of the church or pastor, they are likely to be open to the gospel, at least for a while. Pastors must be diligent in their follow-up and visitation immediately after someone is healed in order to try to share the claims of Christ.

Many pastors shared stories regarding people being delivered from demons. Castino (2001) related that a woman who had been demon possessed for eight months was brought to her by the woman's parents, thinking that she could help. They had been to many witchdoctors, but to no avail. They began to pray for her and, over the course of time, the Lord healed her. Castino then sent two workers to their home and the entire family was saved and baptized. Out of this experience, a new church was born in the woman's *barangay*. In their church planting efforts in this particular *barangay*, they also had a film showing evangelistic crusade and a radio rally and some of the contacts from these meetings were added to the church. Again this shows how the revealed power of the Lord can attract people to Christ.

But as with those who are healed, not all who are delivered from demons decide to serve the Lord. A possessed man called snakes out of the ground and healed people who had been bitten by snakes. However, he had diseased feet. He was healed after the prayer of believers but still continues his pagan practices today. According to Vaden Matiga (2001), who related this story, follow-up was lacking. He also related another story about a teacher, who was a religious woman, who had cancer. She was prayed for and was gradually healed and the next week was riding a motorcycle. During a month of follow-up, she became resistant to the gospel because of the influence of a staunch Catholic relative.

Naomi Besere (2001) told a story about a family who brought a demon-possessed man to her and was delivered. The pastor gave him bread and coffee and claims that this was a major part of his deliverance as he had not been eating and drinking. The man came to church for about three weeks and then left.

Lemuel Matiga (2001) related a story about one witch who had a spirit of witchcraft, which she had received from her father. But she was prayed over and healed. Matiga did not say whether or not she received the Lord, but the point here is that no one is beyond the power of God.

In looking at these stories, one is reminded of the parable of the sower, although the parable refers to the seed as the written or spoken Word of God (Matthew 13:3-9). Sometimes people receive Christ and follow him, other times they do not. Sometimes there was inadequate follow-up and in one case mentioned above, there was persecution within the family. In other cases, people simply were not interested.

But one of the most remarkable aspects of the AG work among the Waray is the fact that many miracles have accompanied the preaching of the Word and God has truly done great things. Miracles get people's attention and draw them to Jesus, the great miracle worker. While the pastors did lament that not all who are healed or delivered were interested in following Jesus, at no point did any of the pastors deny the legitimacy or the value of miracles in their ministry, and they continue to pray for the sick, believing that signs and wonders are an integral part of proclaiming the gospel. With the historical record of what happened now in place, the reasons why the Waray are so open to miracles and the theological issues that underpin their worldview can now be discussed.

Chapter 3

WARAY CULTURE AND WORLDVIEW

The purpose of this review of Waray culture is to provide the cultural and worldview backdrop for understanding the religious attitudes of the Waray and to identify the theological issues which are relevant to them. This then will provide answers, at least in part, to the research questions posed in the introduction.

But both the questions and responses from the research can be broadly applied throughout the lowland parts of the Philippines. Some of the writers quoted in this chapter actually write from a pan-Filipino perspective. The premise accepted by virtually every writer in the field is that because of a common cultural history and a common religion (Roman Catholicism) for more than 400 years, the cultural similarities of the lowland Filipino groups, which include the Waray, far outweigh their differences (De Mesa 1987: Forward). Leonardo Mercado (1994:3) suggests that this may be related to the interconnectedness of the various Filipino languages, given that language, philosophy of life, and worldview, are inseparable.

The contents of this chapter have been drawn from the literature written about the Waray and, secondarily, the literature written by Filipino theologians in subject areas germane to the Waray. Much of the literature regarding the Waray is dated because there was little current work available.

Waray Culture

To understand Waray culture in particular is to at least begin to grasp what they do and why, as well as what they think and feel, including their attitudes towards religion. While a comprehensive study of Waray culture is well beyond the limitations of this study, some important issues must be considered here.

Understanding how Filipinos think is critical to communicating the gospel. Melba Maggay (1999:33), a Filipino social anthropologist, says that Filipino culture is orally based, in spite of the high literacy rate. She explains further:

> In contrast, people in a largely oral society such as the Philippines experience life as primary reality, - [sic] passing events restored in memory and reinterpreted over time; thus the sense that the world is unfixed, a dynamic, interpersonal system of encounters with people and other beings. Thought and expression are often highly organized, but in ways that are imaginative and intuitive rather than analytical and abstract. Concrete human experiences are distilled in proverbs, riddles, myths and parables, thus the cognitive preference for stories rather than abstract words (32-33).

Because of their intuitive nature they may find it hard to articulate their feelings (Beltran 1987:90). Mercado (1994:85) explains that the Filipino uses intuition and induction to reach the abstract (i.e. through poetry) because they are concrete thinkers. David Hesselgrave (1991:325) explains that concrete thinkers tend "to express, inform, and persuade by referring to symbols, stories, events, objects, and so forth, rather than to general propositions and principles." This way of thinking has implications for how a contextual theology can be effectively communicated.

The Waray, like other Filipinos, could be compared to eggs frying in a pan. The separate yokes reflect their individual identities, but their group mentality is revealed in that one cannot tell where the white of one egg ends and the white of another begins. According to Mercado (1994:95), maintaining group cohesiveness is important even, if necessary, at the expense of telling the truth. The Filipino "strives for harmony, but since life is never static, conflict occurs not rarely." The value Filipinos place on being rightly related extends also to the spirit world, which in Waray thinking is integrated with and inseparable from the natural world.

Perhaps no value is greater to Filipinos than family. Here is where most ethical and religious values are formed (Novilla 1971:15). Jaime Bulatao (1992:80-81) writes that the family is the key to the Filipino social structure because one's identity is there. He goes on to say:

> And if the Filipino is sometimes seen as personalistic [sic] and dependent, it may be because he is trying to preserve the structure of a society that values close, interdependent relations. For him to be alone is hell. Heaven to be heaven must contain a lot of loud music and plenty of relatives and friends.

While strong family values are biblical and contribute well to the preservation of society, this can be taken to an extreme. Family loyalty in the Philippines often precludes all other loyalties, even to God. While loyalty to family demands commitment, many Filipinos perceive that loyalty to God does not (De Mesa 1987:200).

Mina Contado (1977) conducted an interesting study of power structures in Waray families in Eastern Samar. She mentions that while her respondents perceived that the husband had more authority, her research suggested otherwise in real practice. According to her, the culturally recognized head of the family, the husband, may or may not be the major decision maker. She discovered that when a typical Waray loves his wife, he will not want to disappoint her and is likely to often give in to her opinions, especially as it pertains to things about the home (1977:34). She also notes that her study was important because of the value of knowing who has the authority or influence when one is introducing innovations, which would presumably include any changes in their religious beliefs (8-9).

The concept of *utang na loob* (debt of gratitude or reciprocity) is an integral value of the Filipino social fabric, involving giving and receiving favors. According to Jaime Belita (1991:39), when Filipinos have such a debt, they feel obligated to express their gratitude by paying it. This mutual reciprocity, then, serves to further strengthen the relationship. Debts of gratitude must be paid or one will be thought of as someone who has no shame (*hiya*) or respect for the feelings of others. However, it need not be paid immediately and there are generally no conditions on how it must be paid (Mercado 1976:65). Julma Neo (1975:49) writes that this debt of gratitude extends to the spirit world. Rituals must be performed for favors granted, whether they are personal or for the community. Also, the concept of *utang na loob* encourages interdependence, which is an essential element in the Body of Christ.

Hiya is a concept that is difficult to translate into English and is hard for Westerners to readily understand. Depending on the context it can be translated as "shyness, sensitivity, shame, timidity, or embarrassment (Bulatao 1992:212). It almost always has to do with "saving face." *Hiya* places a strong emphasis on the development and maintenance of a Filipino group orientation. Bulatao says that *hiya* is influenced by the need to conform to the expectations of one's authority figure or the group of which one is a part. To a Filipino, *hiya* is the most natural thing in the world (1992:213-214). To not have *hiya* is to not be a part of the group and therefore, in Filipino thinking, to be a non-person. To be accused of having no *hiya* is a serious offense.

On the other hand, *hiya* can also be positive. There is a strong interplay between the concepts of *hiya* and debt of gratitude. One's *utang na loob* contributes to the cohesiveness of the group which, as mentioned above, is bound by *hiya*.

Waray Religious Worldview

The deepest assumptions and beliefs about reality lie at the worldview level. This is particularly true with religious views. Robert Schreiter (1985:130) gives an excellent description of the contours of an animist's worldview and belief system, which describes the Waray situation well:

> One cannot, of course, describe the view of the world underlying popular religion [animism] in any exhaustive manner. There are, however, some characteristics that deserve special mention: (a) the world is seen as an interconnected and controlled place. No bad deed goes unpunished, no good deed will be unrewarded, for God sees all. Because of this interconnection and control, there is a limited amount of room for human maneuvering. Some would see this as a certain fatalism about the prospects for human initiative; others, as a way of surviving under hostile circumstances. (b) Concerns are concrete, and requests for divine aid are usually directed at immediate needs. Since the world is a hostile place if one is not protected, a good deal of energy is directed toward assuring continued protection. (c) While concerns are to a large extent concrete, immediate, and this–worldly, there is a balancing concern for death and the afterlife. Death is a major preoccupation because of the high mortality rate in the rural areas. It is not welcomed, except for the very old. Afterlife will reflect how one has lived here, and how one has fulfilled familial and moral obligations.

Because the universe is an interconnected whole, the line between the natural and the supernatural is thin or non-existent. This interconnection, according to Gailyn Van Rheenen (1991:131), includes the extended family, supernatural powers, nature and other humans. Mercado (1992:48) notes that "the Filipino has an incarnational worldview, meaning its perception of the other world and the visible world are very much integrated." He also notes (1975:26) that there is no indigenous word for religion in the Filipino languages. Far from suggesting that Filipinos are not religious, it means that they do not normally cognitively separate the sacred from the secular. In Filipino thinking, these are so blended that some anthropologists cannot differentiate between the two (Mercado 1975:25-26). If this is true, then it follows that living in close harmony with occupants of the other world is critically important to Filipinos.

While most Waray are Catholic, a closer look reveals many animistic practices that pre-date Catholicism and have become mixed with Catholic practices and teaching. Why is this so? Rodney Henry (1986:10) writes that while Catholicism dealt with the issues of ultimate concern, such as sin and salvation, it did not deal with issues of daily survival such as hunting and agriculture. It also did not deal with important every day issues such as the weather, the source of illness and healing and blessing and cursing. Filipinos, however, are aware that Nature plays by her own rules and that these rules are handled by supernatural beings (Jocano 1981:25). Maggay (1999:23) points out the outworking of this belief: "Filipino religion remains primarily a transaction of the powers." The average Filipino, as a result, is at least as much concerned about these spirits (animism) as he is about salvation and sin (Catholicism). Thus these two religious systems have continued to co-exist, intermingled together, described accurately as folk Catholicism, which will be examined more carefully later.

One reason for the resilience of pagan practices may be that they are taught at home. Henry (1986:10) writes that when Catholicism came, the church became the center for teaching Catholicism but in the home the old ways continued to be taught.

Cosmology

Agaton Pal (1956:450-451) provides a useful framework for conceptualizing the Waray view of the spirit world. According to Pal, the Waray spirit world involves four tiers. On the top tier is God, who created the world but is aloof and unapproachable. On the second tier are the Catholic patron saints who intercede before God on behalf of the people for the supply of needs such as rain and good crops. Special masses and all town fiestas are held in their honor. The Virgin Mary, though not mentioned by Pal, should also be placed here. The third tier is what may be referred to as this worldly spirit beings, meaning that they are more likely to be involved in the affairs of people, causing sickness and other mishaps.

In the fourth tier are the *anitos*, the spirits of the ancestors, who are believed to live in unplowed fields and who must be appeased and coerced into leaving before any crops can be planted. Elsewhere I (2000:28) have written that "they are perceived as continuing to play a role in the lives of the living, bringing either blessing or havoc. . . if their needs are not met." *Anitos* are not really dead in the mind of the living. Instead, they exist in another dimension, referred to by anthropologists as the state of the living dead. They remain part of the group and must be venerated.

In truth, while the lines separating these tiers provide a conceptual framework for academic study and analysis, in the everyday life of the Waray, the tiers become intermingled or ignored altogether.

Causality

Waray cosmology reveals a clear cause and effect relationship between the natural and supernatural. The Waray pray to the saints for rain and consult other spirits for healing or for cursing one's enemies through causing illness, misfortune, or even death. Anacion (1991:18) correctly assesses that the Waray's philosophy of causality is the product of their worldview.

Perhaps this is no more true than in issues related to sicknesses. In my previous research we asked the spiritists why people came to them. Some of the spiritists said that people came when their sickness had been caused by a spirit or a sorcerer's curse, the general assumption being that sicknesses coming from the supernatural must also be cured by the supernatural (2000:67).

Because of their beliefs that the spirits are immanent [Pal's third and fourth tiers] and have an impact on daily life, the Waray live with countless taboos and wear various amulets. The taboos have been put in place so as not to offend the spirits and consequently, give them an occasion to cause problems for man. The amulets protect people from the spirits.

Waray causality goes beyond an understanding of spiritual beings. It includes what might be described as spiritual forces as Mercado's (1975:162-163) interesting review of farming practices illustrates:

> In Leyte the farmers have some practices which may seem absurd to foreign observers. In order to have yellow sweet potatoes (camote), the farmer uses yellow clothing in planting. If he wants violet camote, he wears violet clothing. If he wants to have [a] fat camote, he gets a stout man (if he is not stout himself) to do the planting. If he wants camote to have thin skin (which is considered a delicacy), the farmers do their planting naked... Here is not the thought of magic or the like.

Mercado (1975:63) then goes on to suggest that these practices stem from the Filipino view of harmony between man and the elements. This view implies not only that these supernatural forces exist, but that man can manipulate them for his own benefit.

Catholic Folk Practices

From the arrival of Catholicism with Ferdinand Magellan in 1521 until now, Catholicism and animism have been intertwined in a symbiotic, though not always peaceful relationship, known as folk Catholicism. Jadloc (1988:88) concludes that Catholicism modified the worldview of the early Waray and that the interplay between the pagan and Catholic elements have produced the current religious milieu.

Nevertheless, Catholicism has succeeded in becoming deeply imbedded in Filipino culture. Jose De Mesa (1987:181) reminds us that like most people, Filipinos accept their cultural heritage uncritically. In the mind of the average Filipino, there appears to be little, if any, difference between Catholicism and folk practices. Bulatao (1992:6) admits in a non condemning way that after four centuries of Roman Catholicism, "the Filipino is still an animist at heart." According to Maggay (1999:14): "the liturgical synthesis between Catholicism and the indigenous consciousness was unaccompanied by shifts in religious paradigm. The indigenous mind, for the most part, simply assimilated the new elements within its own system."

This assimilation, however, is selective. The inability or unwillingness to sharply distinguish between the elements of folk practices and formal Roman Catholic practices means that one cannot polarize these concepts as sacred and secular (Teleron 1972:134-135). While the rural Catholic may not be well instructed in the doctrines of the faith, he is far from being a blind recipient. Jocano (1981:20) explains further:

> He is also a creative innovator as attested by the way he selects, modifies, and elaborates those elements he draws from the Catholic Church to reinforce the structure of his culturally defined ways of doing things. Thus, in agriculture, for example, we find the use of Christian prayers and ritual objects incorporated in local practices striking.

Since they are adapted and modified according to what the rural Catholic feels that he needs, this suggests that these practices are focused on man, not God and cannot be considered as worship in the classical sense.

Virtually every barrio, *barangay* and municipality has an annual fiesta. Schreiter (1985:129) notes that there is a strong communal aspect in animism and this is evident in the town fiestas. As the word implies, it is a time of merrymaking and the local merchants do good business. While there has been a secularizing trend over the years, no doubt prompting Jocano (1981:42) to write that "the activities clustered around the fiesta are more social than religious," the historical focus has been religious. Among the Waray, the origin of the fiesta often commemorated the arrival of the town's first missionaries, the consecration of a certain church or other place, or a patron saint who warded off danger and pestilence (Mercado 1975:179-80).

In spite of the secularizing trend, the religious element seems to remain strong. Every fiesta includes a religious procession where the saint's image is paraded and honored with devotion (Cesar 1953:49-51). Special masses are said in the saint's honor. The fiesta is also a time of thanksgiving to the saint, believing that the saint is the town guardian and guarantor of its blessings. An excellent example of faith in a patron saint is found among the Waray in Tanuan, Leyte:

> The image [of the Our Lady], believed to be miraculous and powerful, is said to have been carved from a trunk of a '*hamurawon*' tree on the Ambao mountain just on the outskirts of town. It is now a tradition that from the belief and devotion of the people to the Blessed Virgin, the checking up of the approach of three big tidal waves accompanying the destructive typhoon of October 12, 1897, is attributed to the powers and protection of the patron saint - our Lady of the Assumption [italics mine] (Cesar 1953:26-27).

There are a number of theological issues here. Dedication of the fiesta to the patron saint means giving allegiance to that saint rather than to God. This will be investigated in light of the biblical teaching regarding allegiance. If, in fact, the image of the Our Lady of Assumption is powerful, from where does the power come? Also, Mercado (1975:180-181) believes that the theology of the fiesta is bound up with the Filipino concept of non-dualism between the sacred and the secular.

November 1, All Saints' Day, is a national holiday in the Philippines. On this day, families all over the nation may go to the cemetery to visit the graves of their deceased loved ones. According to tradition, the spirits of the dead are believed to return to their graves. Family reunions are held at the gravesite with food offerings being left for the dead, who are still considered to be members of the family. Teleron (1972:116) explains the need for this ritual within the Waray worldview:

> The time when souls of dead relatives and friends are not only prayed for, but also prayed to, supports the function of rituals as communication event for these closely knit families in this world (of the living) and the other world (of the dead). The persistence of offering of food on the graves of the dead asserts the folk belief in the affectivity of such communication. The ritual in the experience of the folk directly articulates the relationship of the living with the dead relatives, as well as the values attached to the life here influencing the hereafter.

Prayer to the dead implies the Waray's belief in the power of the dead to grant or deny their supplications. Leaving food for the dead suggests the Waray's fear that they have the power to impact the living and must be kept happy.

The literature regarding the Waray view of the saints is limited to what is written regarding the Santo Niño de Tacloban, the patron saint of Tacloban City, the provincial capital of Leyte, and to the previously mentioned literature regarding the town fiestas. Other saints, which are prayed to throughout the Philippines, are also represented by various images in Catholic churches all over the Leyte-Samar region, inferring that the Waray viewpoint regarding images is similar to the rest of the country.

The Santo Niño is the image of Jesus as a young boy, perhaps four or five years of age. Mercado (1992:143) explains that the Santo Niño, presented in various forms of dress in various places, is popular because many claims of miracles, including the defeat of enemies in battle and the provision of food. He also mentions that devotees request sin's forgiveness and make vows of what they will do if their petitions are granted. This fits well into the animistic pattern of adoration in return for favors granted and meshes well with the pan-Filipino trait of debt of gratitude (1992:144). While the Santo Niño is popular throughout the country, it is especially venerated in Cebu and in Tacloban City, Leyte where, for more than 250 years, its image has been viewed in an alcove high up in the wall in a church in the heart of the city.

While none of the saints are regarded as omnipotent, all are regarded as being powerful in certain areas. San Isidro, for example, is considered to be the patron saint of the farmers. According to Bulatao (1992:69), these saints are the ones with whom people commune and who live in their consciousness. Faith in the saints, then, gives meaning to people's lives. He contends that the practice of the worship of the saints is justified:

> If these saints thus find their niches in men's hearts and if men's consciousness is thus transformed towards a familiarity with the divine, *who* can, in the overall view, condemn the relics of animism as merely pagan or, even worse, as devilish as the old missionaries did? Let theologians, if they insist, change the names and the formulas in the prayer, but let them keep that divine-seeking process which was in the Filipino from ages ago and which his culture has kept till today (1992:70).

Bulatao appears to be suggesting that "the niches in men's hearts," rather than divine revelation, is the standard by which such practices should be allowed. Whatever one may think of this standard, a question must asked. Why do Filipinos feel the need to worship the saints? Beltran's (1987:130) criticism that fundamentalist preachers condemn the cult of images without understanding why the people do it is, in my opinion, justified. A further discussion about the saints in light of biblical revelation will follow beginning in chapter six.

The issue of saints and the use of images are closely linked. There is an undeniable connection between official Catholicism, which sanctions the use of images, and folk Catholicism. Jocano (1981:23) adds that no image can intercede for the people until it has been blessed by a priest. Beltran (1987:126-127), the most incisive writer on the cult of images in the literature I read, adds that folk Catholicism in the Philippines is impossible to understand without its images. He also explains why this issue cannot be ignored:

> The cult of images is a significant theological issue because sacred images and other forms of religious art can play an important role in bringing believers to a deeper understanding of ecclesial teaching. In the history of the Church, the anthropomorphic representation of the Christ appears to have evolved together with or even prior to the representation of Jesus by symbols. The pictorial language of sacred symbols and representations developed in close connection with doctrinal development, the liturgy and spirituality. Images can render faith accessible to the intellectual process by mediating cognitive comprehension. Reflection on the cult of images in folk Catholicism might help in the search for religious images through which Filipinos can confess what Jesus means to them after having gained insight into, and maintained contact with, transcendent reality through these images (1987:126).

Perhaps these images are revered because Filipinos tend to be more intuitive than analytical. Coming from an aurally based society, what they can see and feel appears to make a deeper impression than what they read. In comparing folk Catholicism with Christology from the West, Beltran (1987:6) holds that Filipinos have an intense desire to experience the extraordinary effects of the supernatural in their lives, as opposed to the Western orientation "towards the cognitive dimension of the faith.". He holds that "images and religious pictures serve less as cognitive landmarks than as evocative objects to arouse religious sentiment. . . . and guide behavior," and goes on to say that "images suggest more than they define" (p. 127). He also suggests that the iconographical form of religious instruction might be more beneficial to the Filipino than logical forms imported from the West (p. 145).

It would be inaccurate, however, according to Beltran, to say that the images themselves are the real objects of adoration (p. 131). The object of devotion is the divine reality represented by the image. In these images divinity can be touched and God is brought near, though in an inarticulate and perhaps indescribable way. Adoration of the images, then, is born from a desire for God's presence (Beltran 1987:130). Mercado (1992:62) explains this by saying: "The holy or sacred for him [the average Filipino] is immanent, so he wipes the statue with his handkerchief. This behavior seems to indicate the belief of the holy as power immanent in the statue." It would seem, then, that the cult of images fits the Filipino worldview well, straddling the line between the natural and the supernatural, presupposing the existence of the sacred realm while remaining anchored in phenomenal reality (Beltran 1987:131-132). Several theological issues come to light that must be addressed in a contextual theology and will also be addressed in due course.

Rituals and Their Roles Among the Waray

Rites and rituals play an important part in the life of the average Waray. From the cradle to the grave, they are surrounded by them, no doubt adding meaning to their lives. Anacion (1991:16) describes ritual as:

> Rituals are prescribed, repeated, and customary activities or ceremonials in a special group. Rituals are closely linked to relationships of the said culture's component. Like art, it greatly affects kinship systems, beliefs, laws and other human habits. Religious rituals, for instance, are closely linked to economic

pursuits which, in turn, are determined by kinship ties and by environment.

The "said culture's component" appears to mean the various aspects of a group's worldview. In other words, rituals function within worldview. Because these rituals are often repeated from generation to generation, they also reinforce that worldview. The link between religious rituals, kinship ties, and economics is keen among the Waray.

Jaime Biron-Polo (1988:27) looks at the sociological perspective of ritual:

> As ideological discourse, this particular symbolic practice addresses the participants both as existential and social constituents and in this social practice, material objects are always important. . . . Moreover, verbal action and gestures in ritual and magic e.g. repetition, shifts in rhythm, specialized vocabulary and changes in pronunciation, are an imperative for efficacy. The specialized ritual vocabulary and grammar are upheld as a language which revered ancestors had created, spoken and therefore generate an awareness of a collective life and history.

Another function of rituals, especially religious ones, is that they help to make sense out of the world. Jocano (1981:43), explains this well:

> The religious rituals in the Philippines viewed from within their cultural context may be described as a psychological construct which underlie the emotional behavior of the people. They make possible the psychical capacity of an individual imaginatively to take situations external to himself into his private experience in such a way that self-assurance is achieved. Without these religious rites, unsanctioned by the [Roman Catholic] Church as they may be, the capacity of the people to have an awareness of their limitation and an understanding of

the 'whys' of society would scarcely develop. For the rural folks, [most of the Waray are rural] the rituals and the basic beliefs surrounding them not only draw together all the separate strands of traditional practices and lore, but also provide the outline from which the people themselves may acquire a clear picture of the way their activities blend with local concepts and an example of the manner in which the practiced rites strengthen the central values of their lives.

How these rites pull together the basic strands of their stories and practices and how they help those involved to have a clear picture of themselves will be demonstrated through a review of various rituals in the following paragraphs. Because the nature of this study is to discover the religious attitudes of the Waray, the meaning of the rituals, their symbols, their purpose, and the source of their power will be discussed. Jocano (1981:25) notes the relationship of these rites in people's lives to their worldview: "to the rural folks there is more to these practices than merely following all the steps in the process of planting; these rites are ways of dealing with the supernatural beings and of coping with events." Many of the agricultural rituals considered here can be done by the landowner themselves, or a friend or relative as well as a *tambalan*.

The purpose of the rice planting ritual is to attempt to guarantee an abundant harvest. In the case of an unplowed field, the spirits of the ancestors who are believed to live there must be appeased before the land can be cleared (Arens 1982:18). Arens explains that elements used in the ritual are believed to be powerful: "A common feature with all rituals is the symbolism expressed in the articles employed from surrounding nature. Formerly a magic power was ascribed to the different articles and it was believed that these articles transmitted certain qualities to the rice by their mere presence" (Arens 1982:11). In this case, the source of the power is not mentioned nor how these qualities were transmitted, but there is a powerful hint here that it must come from some supernatural source. What appears to be important to Arens here is that the ritual was done to improve the quality of the rice.

In many of the rituals reviewed here, there are two variations: Catholic and pagan. While the Catholic ritual gives it new meaning, some of the ancient animistic elements remain noticeable (Arens 1982:3). Arens explains:

> In the christianized ritual the invocations are directed to God and the amulets or charms used now are the symbolic expression of a prayer to God that He may bestow on the rice certain qualities similar to the symbols. In some cases – even in the christianized ritual – farmers still attribute to the charms themselves the power of giving the rice these qualities (1982:4).

He also notes that in this ritual, giving food to the ancestors and other spirits are omitted. He may be suggesting that an effort was made here to contextualize the Catholic faith to the prevailing religious attitudes, as the invocations to God here are normally directed to the spirits who live in the fields. He adds that the symbols drawn from nature have been augmented by religious articles, such as candles and crosses, suggesting that the original intention may have been for these to serve as functional substitutes for the ritual articles drawn from nature. He goes on to admit, however, that in the rural villages, far from the municipalities where Catholicism is much stronger, a syncretism of Catholicism and spirit worship is still practiced. While the people are baptized Catholics, they continue to believe that the spirits are powerful and want to play it safe by sacrificing to them as well.

Not only are rituals used in planting, they are also performed at harvest time. Arens (1982:7) writes:

> After studying reports and observing practices in different municipalities of Leyte it seems that the ritual of beginning the rice harvest can be traced to certain ancient rites of nature worship. Four hundred years of Catholic influence have

Christianized and altered some of the practices through the addition of prayers, the use of Christian symbols, and a shift of emphasis from nature symbols as powerful magic instruments to God the author of all blessings.

It appears evident that while the symbols involved in the ritual have changed to Christian symbols, the meaning behind them and their function have apparently remained animistic. While the motive behind this change may have been sincere, the lack of change in the function leaves its legitimacy open to question, especially in light of the syncretism that has taken place.

Another rice harvest ritual done in some towns is the thanksgiving dinner. This is performed in honor of San Isidro - the farmer's patron saint, the Virgin Mary or deceased owners and tenants of the field (Arens 1982:11). While it is not clear why this ritual is done for the deceased owner or former tenants, unless they are considered *anitos,* doing it in honor of the patron saint or the Virgin is relatively easy to understand. Filipinos believe that the patron saints and the Virgin Mary serve as mediators between God and men. Their view of the supernatural here mirrors one of their cultural practices. In Philippine society, the common man does not talk to high status people directly. He uses a mediator. In the supernatural realm, the patron saints and the Virgin Mary are believed to intercede on behalf of man before God. The concept of thanksgiving, however, is biblical, and many AG churches have annual celebrations to give thanks to the Lord not simply for good crops but for all of the blessings that God gives.

Because the religious practitioners play such a vital role in understanding the Waray worldview, the next chapter takes a closer look at what these people do.

Chapter 4

WARAY RELIGIOUS PRACTITIONERS AND THEIR ROLES

The Waray religious practitioners can be divided into two categories: Sorcerers and *tambalans*, or witchdoctors. They are the antithesis of each other. Sorcerers are feared for their black magic and tend to hide their identity, at least from outsiders, while *tambalans* are well known to all and respected because of their efforts to heal people. Both *tambalans* and sorcerers, however, are in contact with spiritual powers, bridging the small gap between the natural and the supernatural.

Sorcerers and Their Roles

The Leyte/Samar region is known nationwide as a center of witchcraft activity. The belief in sorcerers or witches and witchcraft pervades all levels of Waray society, whether one is in a city or in the rural areas. Most witches do not wish to be known as such. In conducting the field research for my first thesis, we only found one sorcerer that would talk with us. Arens (1982:87) notes that "the life of a suspected witch and her family is made difficult by the constant suspicion of the people. The 'witch' is shunned and sometimes publicly embarrassed." He also adds that witches are believed to be possessed by evil spirits and to possess magical powers (1982:77).

In order to gain the supernatural power associated with being a witch, many go through esoteric experiences. Arens (1982:81-82) explains:

In some places, the power of *barang* is ascribed to witches. *Barang* is the power to inflict harm on persons. Because *barang* results in evil effects, this power has been attributed to witches. It is said that this power was originally transmitted by cave or mountain spirits and fairies. Nowadays, it can also be acquired through the process of *tahas*. Only persons who are brave and have strong convictions can acquire the *barang* power. In order to become a *barangan* (one who has the *barang* power), one must show bravery by going out at nighttime to the cemetery to talk to the dead or by going to the church when the clock strikes midnight.

Mercado (1994:130) adds that sorcerers prepare for *barang* on seven of the Fridays of the Lenton season, the number seven also having some connotation with death practices. If sorcerers are so evil, why do people seek them out and consult them? Nicolasita Cuyco (1983:3) suggests that they are consulted to counteract the black magic of a belligerent sorcerer. Revenge is perhaps the main reason. I have personally witnessed the effect of a sorcerer's curse upon a woman who had failed to pay a debt. The woman's actions suggested that she was not in full control of her mind and the presence of the demonic was obvious, although she was mentally competent enough to refuse my plea to forgive those who had wronged her.

Tambalans and Their Roles

Most of the Waray literature deals with the *tambalans,* whose primary function is to heal. Rebecca Tiston (1982:10), one of the few who have written on the areas of the *tambalan's* call and duties among the Waray, argues for the three classes of these practitioners: *albularyo* (herbalist), the *espiritista* (spiritist) and psychic healer. It would seem better, however, to consider the psychic healer as a sub-classification of spiritist because there is no separate term for psychic healer in the Waray language and because many of their functions are the same.

Some explanation of their roles and rituals will be needed, but issues such as their view of spiritual power and healing will also be considered because of the relevance it has in revealing their worldview. Their belief regarding supernatural power will also be compared to what the Bible has to say about the subject in a later chapter.

Jaime Galvez-Tan (1977:18) explains that the *tambalans* are popular among the Waray and preferred over Western trained doctors because they live among the people, work within their culture, and use remedies and curative materials known to them. When conducting the field research for my master's thesis, we located them by simply driving into town and asking around.

Most *tambalans* are bi-vocational and have no set fee so, in many cases, people come to them because they cannot afford to go to the doctor or hospital. They also fill many other roles in Waray society as psychologist, guidance counselor, diviner, and religious leader (Tiston 1982:9). That fact that *tambalans* communicate with the spirits also gives them authority (Tiston 1982:7). In my previous research (2000:42-43), forty-five out of the sixty-one *tambalans* who answered the question regarding the source of their calling said that it came from a supernatural source. Tiston (1982:13) concurs, adding that the ability to commune with the spirits is imperative to their success. This is significant because the calling of a *tambalan* and their ability to heal are inseparable.

Specifically, a number of them claimed that their call came from God the Father, the Son, or the Holy Spirit, although their concept of the Trinity varies significantly from the Scriptures. In many cases, the call of the *tambalan* proceeds from one generation to the next, although a generation may also be skipped. Receiving one's call from an ancestor is also quite common. Cuyco (1983:30) reports that fifty-seven percent of the herbalists to whom she spoke acquired the work from their parents or other relatives, though she does not say how it was transmitted. Thirteen out of the sixty-one respondents in my thesis indicated the same, although the evidence was generally clear that the call came from *deceased* relatives. Often the call is not negotiable. Normally, a prospective *tambalan* cannot avoid this call without running the risk of being haunted by a spirit the rest of his life (Tiston 1982:14).

Not all feel the call from a supernatural source. Sixteen of the respondents in my thesis indicated no supernatural source of their call. Others mentioned that their call came from the spiritist organization with which they were affiliated. Tiston (1982:13) mentions that some are called by other *tambalans*.

The connection between the call of the *tambalan* and supernatural power is closely related. Once spiritual power is acquired, it must be maintained. There does not appear to be much discussion in the literature on this issue, but it is relevant to understanding the Waray view of how supernatural power is to be handled. Mercado (1992:105) asks if the spiritual discipline of the healers is related to the retention of this power. He then suggests that "the asceticism [which would include rites and rituals] of the Filipino healer seems to be connected with the accumulation of power...."

Many go through an initiation and a period of training before beginning to practice on their own. In many cases, an ecstatic experience marks the beginning of the initiation process, causing a person to put their life in order and live morally. In other cases, the new *tambalan* functions somewhat like an apprentice by learning by rote the prayers that will be used as well as what herbs to use for what disease, in the case of an herbalist (Tiston 1982:14-5). His tutor may be a human or a spirit and his time is spent in preparation for the life of service that he will lead (1982:16).

Tambalans are well known for their genuine care for those who come to them. This care is described by Tiston (1982:12): "he conducts sessions with the patient and relatives whenever necessary as often as twice a week. He holds sessions with them hoping that he will be able to uncover or identify the problem of the patient. He commands the patients to let out the bottled-up fears and anxieties." Elsewhere, she (1977:33) also states:

> The folk medicine user, the faith healer and the *espiritista*, will patiently listen to his patient as the latter pours out his troubles. The *tambalan* is generous and lavish with his sympathy which, as it often turns out, is what the patient needs in the first place. It is even better if the healer has advanced information on the patient's behavioral patterns and symptoms for he can give the diagnosis before the patient begins talking. When he makes an 'educated guess' (which is usually correct) he even impresses his patient more.

In this respect, the function of the *tambalan* bears relationship to that of a Catholic priest who hears confessions, to a Protestant pastor who counsels members of his congregation, or to almost any other kind of care giver. The patient's confessions and sharing are a catharsis for them and, as Tiston mentions above, are a legitimate part of the healing process. However, it should be noted that Tiston also mentions the possibility of the *tambalan* using psychic powers here to influence the patient's thinking and the minds of any others who may be observing (1977:33).

Anacion (1991:23) essentially agrees with Tiston that it is normal for a *tambalan* to listen closely to their patients. Being on the lookout for unusual things that a person might share in order to make a connection to their problem is a common methodology for a *tambalan*. It does not seem uncommon, then, for the *tambalans* to make psychosomatic connections between a person's physical health and their mental or emotional state of mind.

Another role of the *tambalan* is that of appeasing the spirits. The Waray believe that when they are offended, they will cause sickness or other calamity. When these things occur, the Waray often call on a *tambalan* to determine the cause of the problem, which he discerns through divination. Galvez-Tan (1977:11) mentions that this is common in all the barrios. The *tambalan* places food, especially chickens and pigs, where the offended spirits are believed to reside so that they will leave people alone. *Tambalans* also use incantations to appease the spirits. Other roles of the *tambalan* such as divination practices in agricultural rituals will be discussed in due course. However, the main function of the *tambalan* is healing.

Tambalans fall into two categories, the herbalist or *albularyo* and the spiritist or *espiritista*. The separateness of the terms in the language suggests that the local people make a clear distinction between the two. This difference can also be made by identifying their activities. Herbalists use herbs for healing and spiritists may or may not. They are also distinguished by the sicknesses they treat (Johnson 2000:66). If the sickness is determined to have come from the spirit realm, more than likely a spiritist will have to treat it (Tiston 1982:11). It may also be that the spiritists are more deeply involved with the spirit realm, although this difference would only be a matter of degree (Johnson 2000:66).

How the sickness is diagnosed is quite interesting. Many examine their patients much like a medical doctor would. However, the most popular method by far is by checking the pulse (Johnson 2000:59). While this might be part of the way a doctor would investigate the problem, Tiston (1977:19,21) indicates that herbalists take it much further. By examining the pulse's "frequency, regularity, and amplitude in relation to the condition of the body" the *albularyo* or spiritist know whether or not there is disharmony or imbalance in the body and source of the illness. Other methods of divination such as using an egg, supernatural x-ray and the guidance of a spirit, all suggest the involvement of the supernatural (Johnson 2000:59).

When I asked them about how they went about healing the sick, the vast majority reported that they used *orasyons*, otherwise known as "Latin prayers," which are ritual prayers or mantras (2000:64). I have noted that *orasyons* are: "magical formulas that are written on paper in

'Latin' and blessed by the *tambalans* for various purposes. They may be worn, swallowed when diluted in water, placed in bottles or even tattooed on the body, depending on the type of the *orasyon*" (2000:48).

According to Maggay, these *orasyons* can be traced to the time when the Catholic mass was said in Latin, adding that these prayers may represent an early effort at contextualization (Maggay, 2011:161). But the content of the prayers is irrelevant. The *tambalans* of both classes believe that there is power in the words themselves and the simple utterance of them will bring into effect whatever they request.

One of the most common themes in the literature is the spiritist's relationship to supernatural power. The spiritists that I interviewed attributed their power to the supernatural entity that "called" them to their work. According to Mercado (1992:102), the spiritist has a spirit guide "whose function is to teach and to give power and to advise the shaman in his ministry." Tiston (1982:11) agrees that the *espiritista* functions under the influence of a guardian spirit. The influence of these spirits is substantial. Johnson (2000:68) wrote that "the spirit that controls the spiritist dictates what they can or cannot heal, thus the spiritist is not free to choose, even though people come to them for any reason." He also noted that the spiritists cannot necessarily call the spirits whenever they want them to come (p. 84). The controlling spirit sets the agenda.

I found that five of the twenty-seven spiritists indicated that people come to them when they feel that they have been cursed with sickness by a sorcerer or some supernatural entity (2000:68). One spiritist did not appear to make too much distinction between a sorcerer's curse and demon possession (Liguarda 1997).

As with the herbalists, measuring the pulse beat was the most common method of diagnosis (Johnson 2000:70). The same supernatural connotations apply here. Other supernatural methods included diagnosing through the help of the Holy Spirit or other spirit guide, supernatural x-ray, breaking a chicken egg, through a supernaturally empowered ring, through the blessed sacrament of St. Claire and even through a calculator. The connection to the supernatural is unmistakable since the spiritists claim that their spirit guides tell them what is wrong with the patient. While diagnosing by supernatural x-ray, an apparently common method, the spiritists place a piece of paper on the patient's forehead, which may also be anointed with oil and then examines it. The sacrament to St. Claire reflects syncretism with Roman Catholicism and the diagnosis by calculator suggests syncretism with modernity (Johnson 2000:73).

Some spiritists are known as psychic healers. Psychic healers differ from other spiritists because of their ability to perform psychic surgery, which other spiritists admit that they cannot do. Regarding psychic surgery, elsewhere I (2000:83) explained that:

> Psychic surgery takes place when the spiritist is able to put their hands into the body of their patients without the benefit of medical instruments or anesthesia for the patient. This is done without pain during the surgery and no scar remains. But this operation can not [sic] take place without supernatural permission... Nearly all of the psychic healers admitted that this surgery cannot take place without a significant presence of the supernatural. In perhaps all cases, the spirit guide, with the permission of the spiritist, possesses the spiritist's body, and does the healing through them.

While the spirit is working through them, they are in an altered state of consciousness and are not even aware of what is happening. While a complete evaluation of the *tambalan's* level of involvement with the supernatural may be impossible to measure, the level of involvement is probably deeper for the spiritists, especially the psychic healers, than for the herbalists (85-86). There are three reasons why: First, performing psychic surgery requires spirit possession, generally for an extended period of time. Second, more spiritists than herbalists confessed to receiving help from spirit guides. Third, having visited them in their homes, I noticed that spiritists were more likely to have images and other visible religious paraphernalia than did the herbalists.

In summarizing the work of the spiritist in dealing with sickness caused in the spiritual realm, I (2000:77) concluded in my thesis:

> The overtones of the supernatural are again apparent. No one with whom we spoke doubted the power of the spirits or that of the sorcerers to make people sick. Neither did anyone question the ability of the spiritist to correct the situation.

The issues involved here for developing a contextual theology are significant. The nature and use of spiritual power from a biblical perspective as well as biblical teaching regarding healing must be dealt with in order to make the Good News relevant to the Waray. This will be explored further in a later chapter.

In a world full of supernatural beings that must be coerced, manipulated and appeased, the use of amulets and talismans which, according to Anacion (1991:34), are normally made by the *tambalans* is easily understood. The purpose of amulets is to defend against evil spirits, sorcerers' curses and other forms of evil. The Waray conviction that amulets will deliver people from evil is just as strong as their belief in the desire of spirits to harm them. The purpose of talismans, on the other hand, is to bring the person good luck (Arens 1982:107-108). The widespread use amulets and talismans throughout Leyte and Samar is best illustrated by Novilla (1971:107), who notes that every barrio family has at least one.

Power for using these objects is achieved through rituals and maintained through secrecy. Talking about them destroys their usefulness (Arens 1982:119-121). Arens, a Catholic priest, maintains that the inherent power of the charm distinguishes it from the Roman Catholic sacraments which have no power in themselves. However, he freely admits that many of the rural folk are not able to make this distinction and sometimes consider the sacraments as amulets and talismans. He goes on to say that uneducated Catholics feel the same about the scapular (a necklace featuring Christ on the cross) and other medals. In considering what benefits amulets may bring, Arens suggests that psychologically, they give security and at least a feeling of superiority (1957:126). D. J. Sheans, Karl Hutterer, and R. L. Cherry (1970:39) essentially agree, suggesting that they reduce a person's fear of both natural calamity and the supernatural environment.

The Waray view of causality, that both blessing and disaster come from the spirit world, is also clear in the use of tattoos (Anacion 1991:18), especially in the use of a certain kind of amulet known as an *orasyon* tattoo. Anacion (1991:129, 131) notes that the name of Jesus written in the tattoos is used like magic in prayers. The cross also is a common tattoo design. In animism, symbols such as the cross are sought for the magical power believed to be latent within them.

While a tattoo such as the name of Jesus or the cross might seem strange to a Westerner, it is perfectly logical from the Waray perspective. If such an object is indeed powerful, one would not want to lose it, thus justifying it's being tattooed on the body.

Anacion draws a clear connection between the *orasyon* tattoos and the Waray worldview in that the supernatural world can be manipulated by men seeking to control others or seeking to avoid being controlled by them (1991:197). Whether her assessment is true that the *orasyon* tattoo is gradually becoming a thing of the past, she accurately notes that the worldview ideology that undergirds it is not.

The major theological issues here are allegiance and spiritual power. Wearing an amulet, having one tattooed to the back or buried under the house means that one is placing trust in it to protect oneself from hostile spiritual forces. Allegiance is given to whatever works best for the individual. Also, the Waray apparently do not believe that God is all-powerful or amulets would not be necessary. The issue of allegiance will be taken up in due course.

Chapter 5

INTRODUCTION OF THE THEOLOGICAL AND CONTEXTUALIZATION ISSUES

Much has been written on theological issues among lowland Filipinos, mostly from the Roman Catholic perspective. In the first part of this chapter, the theological discussions penned by these authors will be brought to bear on the Waray worldview issues already outlined. This in turn will enable us to identify these issues and provide foundational understanding upon which a contextualized theology can be built. In the second section, the contextualization issues will be presented.

Theological Issues

To construct such a theology, the religious presuppositions of the target audience must be understood. Since the animistic worldview of the Waray is pervasive and encompasses all of life, we will begin here.

Theological Issues Related to Waray Cosmology

Among the Waray practitioners, supernatural beings play a critical role. A clear and understandable communication of the gospel must address the supernatural beings that make up the Waray cosmology from a biblical perspective.

TABLE 5.1
A Comparison of Waray and Biblical Cosmologies

Waray	Biblical
God	God
The Virgin Mary The Saints	No functional biblical equivalent, but connected to idolatry
Various classes of spirits Satan	Angels The Devil Demons
Spirits of the Dead	No cosmological biblical equivalent but related to the activity of demons
Mankind	Mankind

Separating the beings into various categories is helpful for analysis. In reality, however, in the thinking of the average Waray the lines are fuzzy at best, or non-existent. In both cosmologies, God alone is at the top. In the sense that there is none like or equivalent to him, the Waray cosmology is close to the biblical one. But a closer look reveals that their view of God does not quite parallel that of Scripture. Elsewhere I (2000:87) wrote:

> The Waray perceive God, or *Diyos*, to be far off, unknowable, and accessible only through mediaries. According to their belief, he is not all powerful and one cannot know for sure whether or not one is doing his will. The Bible, however, presents an entirely different picture of God. From Genesis to Revelation, he reveals himself as a God who desires to be known.

While Beltran (1987:234) agrees with my assessment that God is perceived as far off, he claims that Filipinos perceive him as merciful and feel he is approachable. For functional reasons, however, they also defer to the Virgin Mary and the saints. In the context of Beltran's entire book it is fair to suggest that he may be saying that the intimacy is felt through the images. Bulatao (1992:73) appears to agree with Beltran, noting that "even the everyday language of the common folk is indicative of this personal relationship with God and the perception of God as present and working in everyday lives."

While God alone is in the top tier of Waray cosmology, the Waray perceive that there are other spirits which work for God. In that sense, then, he is not perceived as being all powerful, although he is certainly more powerful than the rest. Biblical revelation, however, presents a different view which will be articulated later. A major issue for the Waray is God's providence. Does he control the weather, the insects, and the crops? If so, does he do it alone?

In the second tier of Waray cosmology the most important being, the Virgin Mary, is considered to be the mother of all lowland, Catholic Filipinos, including the Waray. She is believed to be the supreme intercessor, a role that is repeatedly reaffirmed in the official *Catechism for Filipino Catholics*, published by the Catholic Bishop's Conference of the Philippines in 1997. It would be difficult to overstate her role in the lives of the Waray who view Mary and the saints as mediators, the Virgin being the supreme mediator. According to the Scriptures, however, Jesus Christ alone fills this role.

The third level in the Waray cosmology is that of the spirits. Many classes of spirits are regarded as capricious and can be either good or evil, depending on the situation or their mood. By contrast, Scripture teaches that the natures of angels are always good and that of demons are always bad, their nature depending on the character of the one they serve. Within this category, the Bible identifies several sub-classifications of demons and regards the devil as their prince.

The Waray worldview, in this respect, is much closer to the biblical view than the mechanistic worldview of the West that tends to deny these middle realms. Van Rheenen (1991:106) notes that "the most overlooked theological issue of the Old Testament among Western theologians is the relationship of Israel to Yahweh and to the gods of the nations." While he does not clearly explain this statement, his entire book is written on the premise that Westerners tend not to see these issues because of their worldview.

However, the roles played by these spirit beings in Filipino cosmology do not necessarily coincide with biblical teaching. The Virgin Mary and the patron saints are believed to mediate between mankind and God. The Bible, however, assigns the mediatoral role to Christ alone, a point I will argue more extensively in chapter six.

Simply stating that the mediatory role is exclusively Christ's, however, is not enough because any contextual theology for the Waray must consider their felt needs. What felt needs do they have that we need to demonstrate can be met in Christ? For example, the Waray pray to the saints for rain which suggests a felt need to appear to have some control of the physical environment. In addition, if it is true that people feel the immanence of God through the images of the Virgin or the saints, what must be done or taught so that this immanence may be felt without the need for images? Of course, if the saints are not who they claim to be, then their true identity must be unmasked, but how does the gospel fill this void?

Demons and other kinds of spirits are also included in Waray cosmology. How do the Waray distinguish between demons and other spirits? The Waray judge the spirits as to whether they are good or evil depending on what they do. But the biblical basis of judgment between good and bad spirits is the source of their power, not their activities (cf. Luke 11:14-28).

The Holy Spirit is also located in the second tier in Waray cosmology. Elsewhere I (2000:27) explained:

> The Holy Spirit is placed here [in the category of the spirits] rather than in the first category because many of the spiritists

with whom we spoke considered his activities to be the same as the other spirits in this category. He is not regarded as remote and does not appear to be worshipped often. Like the other spirits, he can possess the *tambalans* and heal the sick.

I also wrote (2000:89):

> While the research suggests that the Waray regard the Holy Spirit as a lesser being than God [the Father], the evidence in not conclusive, either from the written research or the interviews. . . . However, the issue of spirit possession is extremely relevant to the doctrine of the Baptism in the Holy Spirit and will be discussed here.
>
> The Waray *tambalans* believe that the Holy Spirit, or one of the spirit guides, possesses a person to speak or heal through them... [In one case, we watched as] a spirit took possession of a medium to point out Scripture verses that would serve as the basis for their 'Bible Study' that day. . . .

In the situation mentioned above, I asked another participant what spirit had taken possession of her. I was told that it was either the Holy Spirit, the spirit of Saint Peter or the spirit of a local saint and that this would not be revealed until the end of the session. When I asked whether or not the spirit might lie about it's identity, my informant was adamant that it would tell the truth. But as long as the spirit brings healing to the sick, it's actual identity is irrelevant to the Waray.

What, then, enters the mind of the Waray when they are taught that the Holy Spirit will come upon them (Acts 1:8)? When the Holy Spirit comes, does He leave again just like the other spirits? If not, in what ways is he different? A true contextual theology will answer these questions and challenge the contextualizers themselves to live lives "full of the Holy Spirit and of power."

The fourth category in the Waray cosmology is the spirits of the dead. While many of their activities are the same as other spirits, the difference is that these spirits were once human. The last category is mankind. Far from being isolated from the beings in the other categories, the Waray believe and the Scriptures teach that supernatural beings are active in the affairs of men and women. Conversely then, the actions of mankind, especially prayer and sacrifice, impact the spirit world.

What the Waray believe concerning the theological issues addressed in the field research will be compared to what the Bible teaches on that subject. In cases where the Waray beliefs parallel that of Scripture, contextual points of contact will be much easier. In cases where Waray beliefs are at great variance with Scripture, effort will be made to show how divine revelation may be brought to bear on their beliefs, thus bringing them into conformity with Scripture and changing their worldview.

In the response to each question, the Waray viewpoints revealed by the research must be subdivided into the views of the GP and that of the AG. Both views will be compared with Scripture and the closeness to or distance from biblical revelation on the views of both populations will be noted.

Theological Issues Related to Christology

In reflecting on the issue of Christology among the Waray, both formal and folk Christology must be taken into consideration. We will consider formal Christology first.

Belita (1991:90) claims that a theology of the Incarnation is an important foundation to constructing a biblical Christology:

> To think systematically of Christ in terms of the Incarnation is called Incarnation Christology: Jesus Christ is truly God, truly human, truly one. This is the Church's guideline or parameter for any further discussion on Christ.... The strength of the Incarnation Christology is its recognition of the Incarnation as an act happening at the initiative and will of God.

Belita is correct. Both the fact that the incarnation came at God's initiative and that Christ is both God and man are critical for establishing a contextual Christology. God's initiative in the incarnation reflects his desire to be known and to be on close, personal terms with mankind. Beltran (1987:214) agrees stating that "Christology should expound a theological response that will do justice to the basic presupposition of the Christian conviction that the eternal Son of God became a human being and dwelt among us."

Another crucial Christological issue in the Waray context is Christ's mediation. If the efficacy of Christ's mediation before the Father can be articulated both in theology and in practice, it may then be demonstrated that the mediation of the Virgin Mary and the saints is not only theologically untenable, it is also unnecessary. Arsenio and Edith Dominguez (1989:155) present an excellent argument for the mediatorship of Christ being grounded in the resurrection: "if Christ had not risen from the death [sic], he could not be a qualified Mediator. By virtue of his resurrection he becomes the only true Mediator." In the resurrection, Christ demonstrated his power over sin, death, and the grave, and now, because he is alive, he lives to make intercession for us (Hebrews 7:25).

The cross and the resurrection are critical issues for Christology anywhere, but especially in the Philippines because of the Catholic emphasis on the suffering of Christ (Beltran 1987:162). Here, the significance of Christ is closely tied to the Passover mystery (1987:98). The suffering Christ is also a dominant theme in folk Catholicism. Because of this the resurrection tends to be under emphasized, although De Mesa, a lay Catholic theologian (1987:104,129), does not completely agree. He sees in the resurrection of Christ a victory over the shame of the Cross, a theme that is worthy of further development in Filipino Christology.

In developing a contextual Christology for the Filipino, Beltran (1987:206) warns against being overly articulate:

> Filipinos believe that truth cannot be completely made intelligible by speculative abstractions and metaphysical concepts. Granting that it can be done, human language still cannot adequately articulate what is believed as true. The limits of language, of propositions, and declarative sentences, are not the boundaries of meaningful experience for Filipinos. They are more at home with what lies just beyond those boundaries.

Part of what "lies just beyond those boundaries" are the meanings associated with the images that make up a substantial part of folk Catholicism.

The images of Christ are perhaps the most dominant theme of Waray folk Christology. The sacred heart of Jesus, normally used as an amulet or talisman, can be seen on jeepneys, tricycles, and taxis everywhere. Special focus appears to be given to the images of the Santo Niño. Continuing along his line of thinking that images reflect the theology of the inarticulate, Beltran (1987:129) holds that enculturating these images of Christ is as important as the written doctrines about him. Mercado (1992:147) adds that these images of Christ have helped to emotionally sustain Filipinos in the trials and joys of life.

The Catholic theologians freely admit, however, that there are problems with over emphasizing devotion to the images, although they do not admit to violating the commandment prohibiting images in Exodus 20:4-6. Beltran (1987:137) admits that it is a great error to place inordinate emphasis on the Incarnation and suffering of Christ to the exclusion of his earthly life and ministry. He goes on to add that overly emphasizing the suffering of Jesus will bring on some negative results:

> There is always the danger that in overly emphasizing the suffering and death of Jesus, folk Catholics will lose sight of the final victory guaranteed by the Resurrection. Excessive

concentration on the sufferings of Jesus might foster despair before tragedy, passivity before injustice, numbness in the face of brokenness and the acceptance of alienation as an irrevocable decree of fate. A spirituality of suffering and misery can easily lapse into magic and superstition to control the divine (138).

This magic and superstition are what concerns Dominguez and Dominguez (1989:32). While they appear to concede that there is some theological validity to what the cross and images of suffering represent, they can become magical because they "are thought to convey Christ's taking on himself the weakness of infancy and the sufferings of humanity. The presence of Christ will somehow protect those who possess these symbols." They go on to say that symbols such as the cross are fine when they are interpreted theologically, but become amulets when perceived to be magical and manipulable by people for their own selfish ends. This propensity towards magic motivates them to also say that "the first step in theological contextualization is to shift the prevailing reverence Filipinos have for the magical Christ [who works miracles through images] to the miraculous living Christ as seen in the New Testament" (1989:27).

Dominguez and Dominguez are correct that a biblical Christology in the Philippine context must exalt Jesus for who he is:

> To make Christ preeminent to the Filipinos he must be pictured as the Great Living Spirit which he is. Through his death and resurrection he has been exalted above principalities and powers and any authority and dominion, and above every name in heaven and earth (Ephesians 1:20-21). The concept of this living Christ as the Great Triumphant Spirit that can guide and oversee and keep one from evil spirits should be developed and expanded by the church if we are to make Christ more relevant to the Filipinos (1987:31).

In spite of the biblical prohibitions about idolatry and in spite of his above stated confession that the use of images can lead to "magic and superstition to control the divine," Beltran (1987:130) maintains that "images of Christ can be a valid starting-point for Christology in the Philippines." The best response comes from Dominguez and Dominguez:

> The magical Christ that I once tried to control through symbolism, rituals, externalities, and various forms of worship now becomes the One controlling me. Christ's presence is not dependent on how much one reads the Bible each day. Christ is simply there with him. He can now view life through the living reality of Christ's presence with him. The magical Christ has become for him the miraculous Christ (1987:34).

In his relationship with Christ, it would seem that Dominguez has found the intimacy with Christ that so many others strive for through the veneration of the images. Mercado (1992:147) confesses that "culture being dynamic, the current Bible movement may change the image of Christ in the Philippines." Changing Christ's image according to a biblical perception could mean a thorough teaching on and encouragement to experience the living presence of Christ within the believer. God's image in man (Genesis 1-2), which was marred by sin, now becomes the image of Christ in regenerated men and women who experience and live out the love and character of Christ with one another.

Theological Issues Related to the Religious Practitioners

Several worldview issues related to the religious practitioners were uncovered that must be critically analyzed in the light of biblical revelation. What follows is by no means an exhaustive list of what could be mentioned.

In doing the field work for my previous research, several spiritists spoke of going into an altered state of consciousness (ASC) where they became spirit possessed in order to heal people and deliver messages from the spirit world. Johnson (2000:88) wrote: "the Waray *tambalans* believe that the Holy Spirit, or one of the spirit guides, possesses a person to speak or heal through them. In many cases, this requires the *tambalans* to go into an altered state of consciousness for all or part of the time that the spirit is controlling them." When the healing session or transchanneling is done, the spirit normally leaves.

Bulatao (1992:86), a Catholic priest who is also a clinical psychologist, however, appears to deny the need for supernatural assistance, believing that the human mind, through hypnosis, a form of ASC, is capable of performing the same healing. None of my research would suggest that the Waray agree with him. All of this raises issues related to contextual theology. Where these spirits come from and who they work for are questions seldom asked by the Waray but must be raised in light of Scripture.

On two separate occasions, my assistants and I were able to observe this phenomenon. One of the spiritists was a medium and the other was known as a psychic healer. Beltran (1987:227) explains that cases of spirit possession are common because the sense of individuality is weak. This allows spirits to possess a person through a trance, who then reflects some of the characteristics of that spirit, thus losing their personal identity while in a trance-like state. Bulatao (1992:67) reflects the non-dualistic Filipino worldview when he suggests that the ability to go into a trance is a divine gift, allowing the person to step into the spirit world, which really isn't separated from the natural one. Does the Bible support these viewpoints?

According to Bulatao (1992:85), mediums must go into an ASC before they can give their messages. Mercado (1992:110) adds that after mediums return to a normal state of consciousness, they cannot remember what they said while they were in the ASC, thus differing from the biblical prophets who always remembered what they prophesied or saw in a vision, which could be considered a type of an ASC.

Supernatural power is an issue intricately related to the spirit world. Many of the spiritists who were interviewed in the thesis research indicated that the supernatural entity who called them is also the one who empowers them for service. That the *tambalans* can bring healing is not in doubt. While it may be true that some herbs have medicinal properties and that many of the diseases treated by the *tambalans* would probably heal on their own anyway, there is reason to think that supernatural healing is performed. If so, where does this healing come from? From God? Is it demonic? These issues must be dealt with in order to communicate sound doctrine to the Waray.

While Western theologians have tended to avoid these issues, the Scriptures have a great deal to say about them. Van Rheenen (1991:99) notes that "much of the Bible portrays the struggle of the people of God with animistic powers." A significant writer on these themes is Clinton Arnold (1992, 1996), who makes specific contributions regarding the animistic backgrounds of those living in Ephesians and Colossae in the first century. Much of his exegesis and many of his conclusions, which are pertinent to the Waray, will be discussed in due course.

The Filipino belief in supernatural healing comes from their worldview (Mercado 1992:12). This power is believed to be accessible through *tambalans*. In contrast, the New Testament repeatedly reveals Jesus healing people, demonstrating the appearance of the Kingdom of God in power. This is good news to the Waray. While they appear to limit healing today to the medical profession, Dominguez and Dominguez (1989:29-30) are on target when they write that "the presentation of the living Christ must touch the physical and spiritual needs of Filipinos. . . . Christ, in order to be living and be made miraculous, must still be associated with healing." He goes on to say Jesus' healing ministry was the proof of his authority to forgive sins (1989:31), thus agreeing with Mercado (1992:111) that Jesus was a holistic healer. The source of healing, however, is an important biblical issue, even though it is seldom questioned by the Waray and will be addressed in chapter eight.

Beltran (1987:97) writes that issues of propitiation (or appeasement) and sacrifice are major themes in the Filipino context because of its correlation with Filipino religious expectations. The biblical theme of Christ as the Passover lamb who was sacrificed for our sins may be relevant to the thinking of the Filipino.

Kingdom theology, the teaching of the reign of God in the hearts of men is also relevant to the Waray. According to Van Rheenen (1991:139-140):

> Kingdom theology is appropriate for Christian proclamation in animistic contexts for a number of reasons. First, kingdom theology provides an interpretive model based on the Word of God for explaining the world. Spirit propitiation and appeasement of both malevolent and ambivalent spirits and gods are of the realm of Satan; the worship of awesome, majestic Creator is of the realm of God. . . .
>
> Second, kingdom theology introduces the reign of God, which equips believers to attack and defeat the powers of Satan. By the power of Christ, fetishes and altars are destroyed, Satanic laws overturned, and the spirit possessed healed.
>
> Third, kingdom theology makes no dichotomy between the natural and the supernatural. It acknowledges that the encounter between God and Satan is actively taking place in this world. God heals the sick, blesses and protects his children, and casts out spirits as manifestations of the kingdom. God controls all facets of his world, both physical and spiritual. No dichotomy should be made between these two realms. The missionary working in an animistic society must believe in the reign of God over all domains of life.

Not only does it provide the biblical cosmology mentioned above, the theology of the kingdom teaches that God is a moral being who defines morality for his people and expects them to reflect his nature. This is in contrast to the animistic tendency to define morality by what is best for the individual and to give allegiance to the spirit being who delivers what the people want.

Since the goal of a contextual theology for any people group is to bring them to an intimate and personal relationship with God, issues regarding conversion and discipleship are important here. The core issue of Christianity is allegiance. De Mesa (1987:192) states that allegiance to God must result in total transformation and that to hold back in any area is to short circuit the process. If God demands total allegiance, how does this impact one's attitude toward the Virgin Mary, the saints, and sacrificing to spirits?

The process of how discipleship is accomplished is part of the contextualization issue (Lua 1998:73). As animistic issues revolve around life itself, so also must our efforts in bringing people to the reality of Christ. Lua notes (1998:28) that Jesus' approach to discipleship was life-oriented, taking the disciples with him wherever he went and teaching as the opportunities were presented. She goes on to say (1998:29) that he was holistic, ministering to them spiritually, physically, and emotionally. De Mesa (1987:192) adds that "psychological and socio-cultural health demand a high degree of consistency between belief and behavior. . . ." I am convinced that the Waray need a life-centered approach for evangelism, calling for a triangle of the manifestation of the power of God, teaching sound doctrine, and showing the love of God in practical ways. A more comprehensive development of some of these ideas will be presented in due course.

Contextualization Issues

Contextualization can be defined as the effort to make the gospel of Jesus Christ understandable to people within their own cultural context without distorting the message. There is much more to contextualization than this, but this definition is sufficient for the intent of this study. Both theology and contextualization begin with God and his revelation. To build on anything else is not a sure foundation (Matthew 7:24-29). Maggay (1989:17) agrees that the Bible is "a common text by which theological systems are to be measured and judged." Dean Gilliland (1989:59) notes that however absolute truth may be, it cannot be abstracted from the context in which it is expressed. Theresa Lua (1998:85) explains this by correctly suggesting that "theology is inevitably shaped or conditioned by a set of historical and cultural forces."

To do contextualization, then, requires a strong grasp both of the gospel message and the cultural context into which it is communicated. My interest in this study is to contextualize an initial proclamation of the gospel message to the Waray, with the understanding that much of what is written will be broadly applicable throughout the lowlands.

Cultural Dynamics

One of the challenges to contextualization is that culture itself is an ongoing and dynamic process. While not always simple to define, culture can be explained as "a dynamic system of socially acquired and socially shared ideas according to which an interacting group of human beings is to adapt itself to its physical, social and ideational environment" (Pieris 1989:9). While the meaning of culture must be defined, an overly technical view may cause one to forget that culture is made up of people (De Mesa 1987:205). People, not systems of culture, are the objects of God's love.

G. Linwood Barney, as quoted by David Hesselgrave (1991:103), states that there are four layers of culture that must be understood:

> The *deepest layer* consists of ideology, cosmology and worldview. A *second layer*, closely related but probably derived from the first, is that of values. Stemming from both of these layers is a *third layer* of institutions (marriage, law, education, etc.). This level of institutions is a bridge to the *surface Level* (fourth level) of material artifacts and observable behavior. The artifacts and behavior of the surface level are easily described and even borrowed. Each deeper level is more complex, abstract. It is one thing to describe or share the phenomena of the surface level but it is quite another thing to discover the functional relationship of these to the deeper levels and still more difficult and demanding to decode their meaning at the level of values, ideology, cosmology and worldview [italics Hesselgrave's].

Hesselgrave also notes that because the level of values, cosmology and worldview are more difficult to analyze, many missionaries are tempted to bring change on the surface level only. Biblical Christianity, however, calls for change at the deepest level, thus challenging contextualizers to understand well the culture of the people they are called to serve. Since the religious attitudes of the Waray lay at the worldview level, they were examined in the field research with the intent of bringing the gospel of Jesus Christ to the deepest point of their worldview and bringing cultural transformation through the lives of transformed people.

The Worldview Model of Contextualization

In order to bring about a deep level of personal and cultural transformation, Charles Kraft's (1979) contextual model, known simply as the "worldview" model, was chosen. The reason for choosing this model, as well as his own definition of worldview, is apparent from Kraft (1979:53) himself:

The worldview is the central systematization of conceptions of reality to which members of the culture assent (largely unconsciously) and from which stems their value system. The worldview lies at the heart of culture, touching, interacting with, and strongly influencing every other aspect of the culture. . . .

The position (model) here espoused sees the worldview of a culture or subculture as the 'central control box' of that culture.

This model is chosen, then, because worldview is a culture's driving force. In order for the gospel to really take root in Waray society, it must bring radical transformation. Since worldview drives culture, change must take place at the worldview level which means that understanding how this transformation takes place is critical to seeing it happen. De Mesa (1987:189) explains how Christians can make positive changes:

> When a culture changes, it is actually the set of ideas which the individual shares with the members of his society that changes, naturally, within the context of new experiences. Christians, therefore, as agents of culture change for the well-being of people, set their efforts both on the socially shared mental content in question, especially the worldview, and the restructuring of life in society through movements. It is important to realize this because profound life-giving and life-enhancing changes can be initiated if done within the worldview.

That this change must be done within the worldview of the people in order to be accepted can hardly be overstated. Jocano (1981:67) adds that individuals seldom evaluate things in ways alien to their cultural background, noting that cultural environment influences their thinking, action and sentiments.

Kraft (1979:54-57) lists five major functions of worldview, most of which are relevant to this study: (1) explanation as to how and why things are the way they are, (2) evaluation and judgment of cultural values and goals, (3) psychological reinforcement for that culture, (4) integration of their perceptions of life into an organized design and (5) the idea that no one's worldview is complete, answering all of the questions of life all of the time. These functions will be dealt with in more detail, especially as regarding the Waray, in chapter eleven.

Throughout chapter three, which explained the culture and worldview of the Waray, issues were dealt with that intersect with the various points listed by Kraft. This helped to chart the course necessary in identifying the theological issues relevant to a contextualized theology. As Kraft (1979:57) notes, "members of different cultures arrive at different conclusions regarding reality because they have started from different assumptions." This again shows that those sharing the gospel must be able to identify the worldview assumptions of the people they serve.

In the following chapters the culture and worldview of the Waray will be examined through their responses to a series of research questions designed to reveal their religious beliefs. These beliefs of the general population will then be compared to the responses of Assemblies of God people among the Waray and the Scriptures to further identify the theological issues necessary to a contextual theology. This can then serve as a guide for the effective presentation of the gospel and discipleship among the Waray and other Filipino lowland groups.

Chapter 6

QUESTIONS RELATED TO NATURE AND PRAYER IN TIMES OF NEED

One of the most revealing aspects of a people's religious paradigm is their practice of prayer. Almost all of mankind has a penchant to pray when problems arise. Knowing to whom the Waray pray and why they do it will increase our understanding of their view of God, his power and their own relationship to him. This can then be compared to biblical revelation about him.

Prayer in Times of Drought or Typhoon

Since many of the Waray are farmers, a good point to start in researching their beliefs is nature. The answers to each question will involve a comparison between the general population, known here as the General Population or GP, and the members and adherents (known in the Philippines as sympathizers), or simply AG.

TABLE 6.1
To Whom Do you Pray for Help during Drought or Typhoon?

	GP (460 Resp.)		AG (492 Resp.)	
	Yes	No	Yes	No
1. Pray to the Saints?	391 (82.6%)	68 (17.4%)	50 (10.2%)	442 (89.8%)
2. Pray to God?	459 (99.8%)	1 (.2%)	474 (96.1%)	19 (3.9%)
3. Pray to Mary?	406 (86.7%)	54 (13.3%)	67 (13.7%)	423 (86.3%)

This issue revealed a significant difference between the GP and AG on all questions. That almost all of the GP prays to God comes as no surprise because of the religious nature of the people. What must be considered here is that the vast majority of them also pray to the saints and the Virgin Mary. Why do they pray to all three? First, both the saints and the Virgin are believed to intercede before God in order to secure his favor for the people. Also, the animistic mindset is to get help wherever it can be found. In this case, the issue may be to pray to whoever is necessary to get rid of the calamity and be left alone, meaning that the reason for praying is inherently self-centered.

In looking at the AG results, I have no explanation as to why three point nine percent of the population does not pray to God in time of trouble. This is higher than in the GP. In reality, however, the difference between the two populations is not great.

There is, however, a substantial difference between the AG population and the GP in praying to the saints and to the Virgin Mary, suggesting that as they embrace Christ, they recognize that he alone is all-powerful and can answer prayer. As positive as these results are, however, almost ten percent of the AG still pray to the saints and nearly fourteen percent pray to the Virgin in times of natural calamity. The next table takes a closer look at the AG population's responses to these questions.

TABLE 6.2

To Whom Do the AG Pray for Help during Drought or Typhoon?

	Members (425 Resp.)		Adherents (67 Resp.)	
	Yes	**No**	**Yes**	**No**
1. Pray to the Saints?	11 (2.6%)	414 (97.4%)	39 (58.2%)	28 (41.8%)
2. Pray to God?	408 (95.8%)	18 (5.2%)	66 (98.5%)	1 (1.5%)
3. Pray to the Virgin Mary?	20 (4.7%)	403 (95.3%)	47 (70.1%)	20 (29.9%)

On questions one and three, the differences between the members and adherents were significant. On the second question, the frequencies expected were too small for chi-square analysis.

The responses to questions one and three reveal that the adherents are much more likely to pray to the saints or the Virgin Mary than the members. The same is true with question three, reflecting the need for greater maturity. Comparison between the members and the adherents by percentage for the second question reveals that their attitudes in regards to praying to God are close, which is not surprising.

Before You Plant Crops, Do You Have a Witchdoctor or Someone Else Come and Perform Rituals or Sacrifices?

Just over half of the GP respondents plant crops. Among the AG, the number is just over one third. Those who planted crops were then asked if they had rituals performed. Only thirteen percent of the GP and three point nine percent of the AG said yes, revealing that the GP are more likely to be involved in rituals. The small GP percentage suggests, however, that perhaps this is not a major issue to them. That even a small percentage of Assemblies of God people do this, however, is cause for concern.

Only one of the 150 AG members said that they had rituals performed as compared to six out of twenty-eight adherents who indicated that they did so. When asked why they do these things, most of the GP and the AG said that the purpose of rituals is to ensure a bountiful harvest, which requires driving away evil spirits and appeasing the spirits of the ancestors.

Using rituals to insure a bountiful harvest or to keep away insects and evil spirits can only mean that the people see a supernatural causality, a connection between supernatural beings and their world. As with all of the questions, the respondents were given the opportunity to list other answers. Nine of the GP named various saints or spirits of the dead, to whom they presumably pray. Two stated that they were just following their traditions, one mentioned superstitions and one said they perform rituals to ask for mercy. The goal here is good crops and they do whatever must be done to achieve that purpose.

All 149 AG members who did not have rituals performed and all but one of the twenty-two adherents said that they pray to God, which is not surprising. For question three the difference between the two groups was significant. The responses here do reveal that the adherents are much more likely to pray to San Isidro, the patron saint of the farmers, than do the pastors and members. That eleven of the members and thirteen of the adherents pray to the Virgin Mary, however, is cause for concern. Those who do not do rituals were asked if they did anything else.

TABLE 6.3
Actions Done Instead of Rituals

	GP (224 Resp.)		AG (171 Resp.)	
	Yes	No	Yes	No
1. Have the pastor or priest come and dedicate the crop?	17 (7.6%)	207 (92.4%)	39 (22.8%)	132 (77.2%)
2. Pray directly to God and dedicate your crops to the Lord?	216 (96.4%)	8 (3.6%)	170 (99.4%)	1 (.6%)
3. Pray to San Isidro?	183 (81.7%)	41 (18.3%)	24 (14%)	147 (86.%)

The differences between the GP and the AG were significant on questions one and three. In question two, the frequencies expected were too small for chi-square analysis. While the AG people are more likely to call on a pastor to pray over their crop, that only seven point six percent of the GP and only twenty-two point eight percent of the AG actually do so may suggest again that this is not a particularly important matter to the majority of farmers.

Regarding prayer to God, the AG people are slightly more likely to pray than the GP. Both populations, however, exhibit a strong belief that God is active in the affairs of men, and that he has influence over the natural elements. Where the populations differ substantially, however, is in regard to praying to the San Isidro. The overwhelming majority of the GP does pray to him, while the percentage of the AG people who do the same is comparatively small. Generally speaking, the saints are perceived to be closer to the people than God himself, which may mean that people are more comfortable in praying to them.

A Question About Prayer in Time of Need

While there is some overlap with the previous question about prayer in times of drought, this question was designed to cover the wider needs of the Waray.

TABLE 6.4
To Whom Do They Pray in Times of Trouble?

	GP (461 Resp.)		AG (492 Resp.)	
	Yes	No	Yes	No
1. To God or Jesus?	459 (99.6%)	2 (.4%)	492 (100%)	0
2. To the Virgin Mary?	409 (88.9%)	51 (11.1%)	58 (11.8%)	433 (88.2%)
3. To the Santo Niño?	400 (86.7%)	61 (13.3%)	50 (10.2%)	439 (89.8%)
4. To other saints?	236 (51.5%)	222 (48.5%)	22 (4.5%)	465 (95.5%)
5. Anyone Else?	13 (2.8%)	445 (97.2%)	3 (.6%)	478 (4.6%)

According to question one, almost all of the GP and AG pray to God in time of need. The other responses, however, reveal responses similar to those in Table 6.1 on page 87 regarding the need to control the crops.

But why do they pray? In answering this question, between ninety-four and ninety-seven percent of the GP said they pray to God, Jesus, the Virgin Mary, and the saints to control the weather and drive away evil spirits. This is the same animistic philosophy that undergirds the felt needs for planting and harvesting rituals.

In looking at the question related to God, both sample populations believe that God has at least some control over the weather and they pray to him in order to make sure the weather benefits humanity. They also almost equally believe that God is able to drive demons away. The answers to both of these questions indicate that, in both groups God is powerful. The a high degree of agreement between the GP and the AG regarding prayer is important for presenting the gospel to the Waray, an issue that will be discussed in due course.

But the similarities end here. The data in the other responses indicate that the GP respondents feel that they can pray to any supernatural being regarding these issues. Among the GP the percentages in the responses to questions to two to four suggests that the GP sees no functional difference between God and the saints, and reflects the GP's desire to control their environment, both in the natural and supernatural realms. Their felt need to pray to beings other than God suggests two possible views: God is not all powerful or that they are more likely to get what they want if they use an intermediary.

In looking at the AG responses, however, the vast majority pray to God alone, apparently feeling no need for the others. Assuming that the AG would have shared the same values that the GP reflect before they came to Christ, this fact is evidence of a real paradigm shift in their thinking. When they were invited to give additional answers, many reflected that God could help because he is all-powerful, and the Creator and sustainer of all things. However, this table reveals that there is a small minority of the AG respondents who continue to reflect their former religious tradition just as they did in Table 6.1 on page **87**. Why this is true will become clear when the responses of the members are compared to that of the adherents.

TABLE 6.5
To Whom Do the AG Pray in Times of Trouble?

	Members (425 Resp.)		Adherents (67 Resp.)	
	Yes	No	Yes	No
1. God or Jesus?	425 (100%)	0	67 (100%)	0
2. The Virgin Mary?	15 (3.5%)	410 (96.5%)	44 (65.7%)	23 (34.3%)
3. The Santo Niño?	10 (2.4%)	413 (97.6%)	40 (60.6%)	26 (39.4%)
4. Do you pray to other saints?	2 (.5%)	420 (99.5%)	20 (30.8%)	45 (69.2%)

The responses to question one are nearly identical. In the responses to questions two through four, however, the adherents, similarly to what they did in Table 6.2 on 88, revealed a much higher tendency towards praying to someone other than God. They reflect values closer to the GP here than to those of the members. This suggests that many still have not seen the need for change in this area of their lives. Again, however, the critical question is why.

TABLE 6.6
Why the AG Prays to Supernatural Beings

	Members		Adherents	
	Yes	No	Yes	No
God or Jesus	425 (Total Resp.)		67 (Total Resp.)	
1. Because he can control the weather?	423 (99.5%)	2 (.5%)	64 (95.5%)	3 (4.5%)
2. Because he can drive away evil spirits?	423 (99.5%)	2 (.5%)	61 (91%)	6 (9%)
The Virgin Mary	15 (Total Resp.)		43 (Total Resp.)	
1. Because she can intercede before God?	14 (93.3%)	1 (6.7%)	39 (90.7)	4 (9.3%)
2. Because she can control the weather?	12 (80%)	3 (20%)	36 (83.7%)	7 (16.3%)
3. Because she can drive away evil spirits?	13 (86.7%)	2 (13.3%)	36 (83.7%)	7 (16.3%)
Santo Niño	10 (Total Resp.)		40 (Total Resp.)	
1. Because he can intercede before God?	10 (100%)	0	36 (90%)	4 (10%)
2. Because he can control the weather?	10 (100%)	0	35 (87.5%)	5 (12.5%)
3. Because he can drive away evil spirits?	10 (100%)	0	36 (90%)	4 (10%)
Other Saints	2 (Total Resp.)		20 (Total Resp.)	
1. Because they can intercede before God?	2 (100%)	0	18 (90%)	2 (10%)
2. Because they can control the weather?	2 (100%)	0	17 (85%)	3 (15%)
3. Because they can drive away evil spirits?	2 (100%)	0	16 (80%)	4 (20%)

While the numbers are not large, the motif, especially among adherents, that one can pray to various supernatural beings is consistent, reflecting a lack of growth and maturity.

What Does the Bible Say?

Three critical theological issues arise out of this research on prayer and rituals regarding the weather and crops: providence, blessing and cursing, and divination. The theological question behind prayer in time of need is spiritual mediation.

Providence

The critical issue in relation to weather and crops is providence, God's governance of the created order. In this case, the views of the GP and AG will be examined here in light of God's ability to control such things as the weather.

The vast majority of the GP respondents pray to God, the Virgin Mary, and the saints. The respondents indicate their belief that God, the Virgin, or the saints are all capable of sending rain. The GP view acknowledges that God controls the elements but fails to acknowledge that he alone does so. The GP then view God not as all-powerful, but as someone who shares power with others.

By contrast, the AG people showed markedly less interest in praying to the saints or to the Virgin for any reason. Most of those who continue to do so are adherents. Since they are almost always new believers, this is not surprising. What is noteworthy here is that there is a transformation in process in the AG people's thinking. As they study the Bible and grow in their experience with God, their thinking and their practices reflect an increasing trust in God who, in his providence is in control of what he created and who can and should be appealed to for help.

God is the creator of all. Henry Thiessen (1979:119) writes: "God, as creator of all things visible and invisible, and the owner of all, has an absolute right to rule over all (Matthew 20:15; Romans 9:20ff.) and he exercises this authority in the universe (Ephesians 1:11)." Not only did God create the world, he continues to preside over it as the doctrine of providence teaches. Thiessen (1979:120) notes:

> The Scriptures teach that although God rested after he had completed the work of creation and had established an order of natural forces, he yet continues his activity in upholding the universe and its powers. Some Scriptures speak of [Christ's] preserving activity in a comprehensive way. For example, [You] alone are the Lord. Thou hast made the heavens, the heaven of heavens with all their host, the earth and all that is on it, the seas and all that is in them. Thou doest give life to all of them' (Neh. 9:6); 'He is before all things, and in Him all things hold together' (Col. 1:17); 'And He is the radiance of His glory and the exact representation of His nature, and upholds all things by the word of His power' (Heb. 1:3).

To quote from Thiessen (1979:123) again:

> Scripture indicates that God controls all the physical universe. Sunshine (Matthew 5:45), wind (Ps. 147:8), lightning (Job 38:25, 35), rain (Job 38:26; Matthew 5:45), thunder (I Sam. 7:10), snow (Job 37:6); 38:22), and frost (Ps. 174:16) are all subject to his bidding. The heavenly bodies, such as the sun (Matthew 5:45) and the stars (Job 38:31-33), obey his will. The mountains are removed (Job 9:5), the earth quakes (Job 9:6), and the ground yields her increase (Acts 14:17) at his mandate. He uses the beneficent elements as expressions of his goodness and love, the destructive as instruments of discipline and punishment. Men should, therefore, humble themselves in the times of physical visitation and pray to him who has all the elements in his power.

All of nature, both the animate and inanimate, was created by God and continues to be under his complete and sovereign control.

CHAPTER 6 ❖ 97

Nowhere in these Scriptures does God delegate this authority to anyone else. The Scriptural view of God's providence is that he holds all things in his hands (Colossians 1:17; Hebrews 1:3), sharing neither his power nor his glory with any other, nor needing help from anyone.

In comparing the Waray views to the Scriptures, the GP view falls considerably short of God's revelation because in it God is not all-powerful, apparently not having total control of the world. The AG population reflected a much more biblical viewpoint by indicating that, for the most part, they pray to God alone. This gives evidence that the pastors are teaching their people about God's providence, that one can and should look to him for all things and they are experiencing his care, which helps them adopt new values and put away the old practices.

God's providence is also the biblical issue behind the question, "Before you plant crops, do you have the witchdoctor or someone like that come and perform rituals or sacrifices?"

At the heart of this issue is supernatural causation. There is ample evidence that the Waray believe that supernatural forces have a role to play in the success or failure of growing crops. While there are only a comparative few that have specific rituals done, the vast majority of the GP pray to God and San Isidro. That they pray to both is again indicative of animistic thinking that allows them to pray to whoever will give them what they want or need. This also reveals a belief that God shares his power.

A few Waray, because of their belief in supernatural causality, believe that insects, set in motion by demonic forces and malevolent ancestors to bring curses must be appeased. In this case, there is no thought of obedience to God, but only appeasing supernatural forces in order to be left alone to have a good harvest. Some of the AG people said they would ask their pastor to pray over their crops, suggesting that they believe in God's power to bless them. However, only thirty-nine of the 178 AG respondents who plant crops indicated they do this, which is not a substantial number.

The AG respondents, in comparison with the GP, focus their prayers on God alone, suggesting that they may understand that only God can help them and perhaps that he desires to bless them. That fourteen percent do pray to the San Isidro is again evidence of a need for more teaching.

Blessing and Cursing

The biblical concept of blessing and cursing relates back to the doctrine of providence. God's providence is expressed through his absolute ability to control the crops. It also establishes the fact that he *alone* handles these things, thus revealing the San Isidro as an imposter and false god. It can be said that the GP are correct in their perception of supernatural causation but fail to recognize that God, not the spirits or the saints, bring the blessings or curses.

Furthermore, in the Waray view, blessing and cursing may come from a variety of supernatural sources and these sources must be appeased through sacrifices in order to assure a bountiful harvest. These sacrifices and prayers, however, as mentioned earlier, are self-centered. The focus is on acquiring blessing without the thought of God, who alone brings blessing and cursing. The GP also gives no thought to appealing for God's blessings by living in obedience to his word. The essential difference here, then, is in the lack of the GP's understanding of God as creator and sustainer of all things, and God as judge of the thoughts and activities of mankind.

In the Scriptures blessing and cursing comes from God who will bless the crops, depending on the obedience of his people. On this issue, the Old Testament has a lot to say. Deuteronomy 28:1-6 states that God would bless the children of Israel with material abundance if they obeyed. If they did not obey, disaster would be the result (Deuteronomy 28:15-24). While these verses specifically relate to God's relationship with Israel, the prophets of the Old Testament proclaimed God's judgment on the nations because of their sin (cf. Isaiah 13:15-21,

23-24; Jeremiah 46-51). There is abundant evidence of God's ability and willingness to reward obedience with blessing or disobedience with cursing in Deuteronomy 28, as well as elsewhere in Scripture. In this case, however, God issues a challenge to his people to walk in obedience and see what he will do as a result. The implication is clear that God desires to bless those who trust in him.

Divination

While it is true that not many of the Waray have rituals performed, that even some of them do so means that this issue must be dealt with in light of the Bible. Most, if not all of these rituals, fall under the classification of divination. David Aune (1979a:971) defines divination as "the art or science of deducing the future or the unknown through the observation and interpretation of some facet of nature or human life, ordinarily of an unpredictable and trivial nature." Walter Liefield (1976:146-147) mentions several of the numerous kinds of divination: Chresmology (prognostication by seers), oneiromancy (the interpretation of dreams), astrology, necromancy (consulting the dead), and mechanical means (the observation of water, fire, casting of dice, rods, or arrows). Aune (1979a:974) adds two more: Teraphim (cultic images i.e. Laban's household gods in Genesis 31:34), and predetermined signs or omens (i.e. Gideon's fleece in Judges 6:36-40).

Leviticus 19:26, 31, and 20:6 specifically condemn divination and sorcery and command people not to consult spiritists and mediums. The severe punishment for doing so indicates that God will curse those who practice such things, especially false prophets who prophesy by divination (Jeremiah. 14:13-16). In Deuteronomy 18:10-13, Moses declares that divination, along with witchcraft, sorcery, interpreting omens, casting spells, necromancy and consulting spiritists and mediums are an abomination to God. In 1 Samuel 15:23, divination is pared with idolatry. In Isaiah 8:16-20, practicing divination, in this case, necromancy is condemned because it is done instead of inquiring from God who, in the Old Testament, regularly spoke through his prophets. The conclusion can be drawn that divination is wrong because it denies God his rightful place in the lives of people. In other cases, prophecies given by divination directly contradicted what God had already spoken and were given to tell the people what they wanted to hear (cf. Jeremiah 14:13-16; 27:8-11; Ezekiel 13:6-9). God condemned these false prophets because they intentionally misled the people regarding the judgment on them that God had already decreed.

Not all forms of divination, however, are necessarily condemned in Scripture and, in some cases, God actually revealed his will through them. Aune (1979a:972) mentions specifically that interpreting dreams and casting lots are given tacit approval in the Bible, suggesting that these may be allowed as long as they acknowledge God as sovereign and active in the affairs of men (cf. Proverbs 16:33; Acts 1:23-26). There are many examples in Scripture of dreams that were used to glorify God (i.e. Genesis 41). In this case, as well as others that could be mentioned, God actually used dreams to send messages to people. Liefeld adds that prognostication by seers was employed in the Old Testament in order to ascertain God's will (I Samuel 9:9). He does go on to say (1976:146) that according to Micah 3:7, the practice of the seer is not always accepted by God.

A case of using a predetermined sign is found in Judges 7:4-7, where God tells Gideon how to determine who will participate in his strike force and who will not, depending on how they drank water (Aune 1979a:974). In this case, again, however, divination was used to determine the will of God.

Another case of legitimate divination in the Bible is the Urim and Thummin. Although their appearance and exact usage is not known, they were kept in the breast piece of the ephod of the high priest (Exodus 28:30). Moses directed that it be used to determine the will of the Lord (Numbers 27:21). In 1 Samuel 23:9-12, David used it in such a way that required only yes or no answers to the question of whether the people he was currently staying among would turn him over to King Saul. In this case, he used it to determine what people would do, not to find out the will of the Lord, but God still answered him.

In these examples, divination was allowed because it helped to determine the will of God, giving God his rightful place at the center of the lives of the people involved. In comparing this to the Waray's use of divination, it can be concluded that the Waray's use of divination is wrong because it is focused on getting people what they want, and dishonors God by not considering his will.

Spiritual Mediation

As the survey revealed in Table 6.4 on page 91, all but two of the respondents pray to God or Jesus, making a tremendous statement about the Waray's belief in the power of prayer. While conducting my previous research among Waray witchdoctors, sixty-nine out of the seventy allowed me to pray for them at the conclusion of the interview. One can safely assume that almost all Waray inherently understand the value of prayer in tapping into supernatural power.

But in looking further at Table 6.4, some significant differences are apparent between the two sample populations as the vast majority of the GP also pray to other supernatural beings.

In praying to the Virgin Mary, the Waray are much like the other lowland Filipinos. Mary is considered to be the mother of the Filipinos and is widely venerated. The CBCP (1997:16-17), the authoritative voice of Roman Catholicism in the Philippines, endorses prayer to Mary:

> The typically "Filipino" approach to Christ, therefore, ***is with and through Mary***. Devotion to Mary has always been intimately intertwined with Christ... Marian devotion and piety seem co-natural to us Filipinos. Mary is deeply involved in each of the five Filipino characteristics leading us to Christ. The 'family altar' in so many Filipino homes witnesses to ***Mary as mother of Jesus and our spiritual mother***. Thus she is at the

center of our *family orientedness*. As *celebration* and *meal-oriented*, Mary's month of May is noted for the fiestas in her honor and pilgrimages to her shrines. For *suffering in life*, Mary is venerated as the Mater Dolorosa, the sorrowful Mother, who's '**Perpetual Help**,' compassion and love is sought through popular novenas and devotions. As *bayani-oriented* [hero oriented], we have Mary as our **Queen**, the loving mother of Christ our king. Moreover, she is the young maiden *whose life commitment*: 'Be it done to me according to your word,' is repeated thrice everyday in the Angelus.

Again, the issue of honoring culture and Catholic tradition over the Scriptures is evident here. Mary is the mother of Jesus and, like any good son, he would want to be obedient to his mother. The Waray, like other Filipinos, believe that for this reason, as well as for the other qualities noted above, Mary is an excellent choice to serve as mediator because she is believed to help the people get what they want from God.

Devotion to Mary is strong in the Philippines for two reasons. One, Catholicism came there from Spain, which is a stronghold of Marian devotion. Second, the idea of having a strong but loving mother is familiar to Filipinos as Filipino society as a whole, including the Waray, is almost a matriarchal society.

The other features of Filipino life, mentioned by the CBCP above, also fit well with Marian devotion. As the Waray are a people who love good food and loud music, fiestas dedicated to the Virgin mesh well in Waray society. As the mother who stood at the foot of the Cross and watched her son die, she is believed to understand well the sufferings of the poor and disenfranchised Waray. *Bayani*, referred to above, is the root word in Tagalog, the national language, for hero. Because of her perceived maternal qualities and the fact that Filipino society generally places a high value on the role of women, Mary is their heroine. From the data reviewed here, nearly all of the GP believes that she is a wonderful intercessor, powerful and able to help. Here, a real love relationship between Mary and the worshiper cannot be denied, although the worshipers are still known to pray for selfish reasons. But can Mary or anyone else answer prayer?

The legitimacy of Christ's mediation is not questioned by the Waray. Therefore, the focus of the study here will be on whether he is the only mediator, or whether the Virgin Mary and the saints have a legitimate claim to that role. To answer this question, the biblical qualifications of a mediator must be established.

Ronald Wallace (1986:303) notes that the New Testament, building on the concept of the covenant in the Old Testament, "places the mediating work of Jesus Christ in the context of fulfilling the covenant's terms. Hebrews especially describes Christ as the mediator of the 'new and better covenant' (Hebrews 8:6; 9:15; 12:24)." This new covenant involves a relationship between God, who is holy and mankind, which is sinful. Christ Jesus, God in human flesh, stands in the middle (1 Timothy 2:5-6).

In Christ's life and teachings, glimpses of his mediation appear. In John 14:13-14, he teaches that we should pray to God the Father in his name. In John 14:6, Jesus claims to be the way, the truth and the life, adding that he is the only way to the Father. In Acts 4:12, the Bible teaches that we can be saved only by calling on the name of Jesus, noting that there is none other name, power or entity that can save us. Nowhere in the Bible are people ever encouraged to pray in the name of any other. Jesus Christ is the only mediator. The first actual example of Christ's ministry of mediation is his high priestly prayer in John 17, where he interceded specifically for all believers. He offered this prayer the night before his crucifixion, the ultimate act of mediation.

The Bible clearly teaches that the purpose of the cross is for mankind, separated from God by sin, to be redeemed and brought back to God (2 Corinthians 5:18). The entire passage of 2 Corinthians 5:11-21 centers on the idea of estranged man being reconciled to a holy God who cannot ignore sin, with Christ Jesus standing in the gap as the mediator. Drawn from the analogy of the Old Testament sacrificial lamb, which had to be perfect, without blemish, the mediator between God and man had to be sinless. Second Corinthians 5:21 indicates that Christ had no sin, therefore he qualified as mediator. Since he alone had no sin, he alone is qualified. The Roman Catholic teaching that Mary also had no sin is not found in the Scriptures.

A key passage related to Christ's mediatorship is I Timothy 2:5-6. In attempting to buttress his argument for a biblical basis for the mediatorship of Mary, Eduardo Arellano (2001:210) interprets this passage to mean that there can be more than one mediator:

> But the unique mediation of Jesus Christ, precisely in its divine and human perfection, allows others to participate and share in this one source of mediation to the Father. The Greek word used for 'one' in the Pauline text of I Tim. 2:5-6 is '*heis*' which means 'one,' 'first' or, 'primary.' This does not in any way stops [sic] sharing of mediation with others.

This interpretation has several problems. While the word *"heis"* can mean "more than one," it can also mean "'single,' 'once-for-all,' 'unique,' or 'only,' or ... 'only one,'" suggesting that the semantic range of this word is rather wide (Stauffer 1964:434). Therefore, while lexicography does help determine the meaning of the word, the exact meaning of the word must be determined by its usage within the context of the passage. A syntactical analysis of the sentence where the phrase "one mediator" appears specifically reveals that this "one mediator" is none other than "the man Christ Jesus, who gave himself as a ransom for us." Clearly "one mediator" can only refer to Jesus Christ. No other mediator is in view here.

The book of Hebrews contains the bulk of Scriptural teaching regarding the high priestly ministry of Christ. Addison Leitch (1976:153) notes that one of Christ's mediatory roles is as a vehicle of God's revelation (Hebrews 1:3). In the Old Testament, God spoke through prophets and others, but now, in the New Testament, God has spoken to us through Christ. Hebrews 1:1-3 makes a clear statement regarding the deity of the mediator.

Beginning with 4:14, however, his humanity begins to appear. The phrase, "who has gone through the heavens," suggests his transcendence (Bruce 1964:85). The author of Hebrews here is hinting at the divinity of Christ, who then became flesh (cf. John 1:14). Because he was human and, therefore, tempted in ways such as we are, he can understand our weakness and our challenges in life. F.F. Bruce (1964:86) aptly notes that because Christ was sinless and bore the trials of the sinful, he endured trials that were greater than ours. Along with stating his suffering and struggles, Hebrews is also quick to reaffirm that he was sinless (Hebrews 4:15). To have sinned at any point in his life would have disqualified him to be the mediator.

Because of Christ's mediatorship (Hebrews 4:16ff.), believers can approach God's throne in confidence that God will hear the petitions of their hearts and render help in time of need. William Lane (1991:123) notes that having a mediator who can readily identify with the struggles of mankind is a powerful incentive to pray. The Waray feel that Mary identifies with them in their struggles and privations in life. But since Mary is not transcendent, this passage cannot refer to her. This is another reason why the Catholic claim to the legitimacy of her mediatorship is not biblical.

The Hebrews 8:6-13 passage refers to Christ as the mediator of a new and better covenant. He did so by way of the cross. In 8:1, the deity of the mediator is again mentioned. No one else has the authority to occupy such a high position.

In summary, the qualifications of a mediator are deity and sinlessness. Only Jesus Christ is qualified. In comparing the Scriptures above to why the Waray look to Mary, it is easy to see that a properly taught theology of mediation would demonstrate to the Waray, especially the GP, that Christ is loving, compassionate and understanding, just as the GP perceive the Virgin Mary to be. Because the mediation of Christ is complete, there is no need for another mediator. Jesus is sufficient to meet the real and felt needs of the Waray, as the AG population has already discovered.

Understanding the Waray views regarding nature and Mary's and the saints' alleged abilities to mediate and control the elements of nature, as well as what the Bible says about these beliefs must shape our the proclamation of the gospel and the discipleship process. The following chapters consider other roles that Mary and the saints are believed to fulfill among the Waray.

Chapter 7

QUESTIONS RELATED TO ROMAN CATHOLICISM

Roman Catholicism has dominated the religious landscape of the Philippines for more than 400 years. Over the process of time, not only did it shape and change the animistic practices that preceded it, these practices also molded the practice of Catholic faith. When Catholicism arrived, the saints simply supplanted the spirits that the Filipinos already worshiped. The result was a syncretistic blend in the daily life. Nowhere is this syncretism more evident than in the celebration of All Saint's Day and the town fiestas. These two significant Roman Catholic celebrations are the subject of research and comparison here with biblical truth about idolatry and the spirits of the dead.

Do You Go to the Gravesite on All Saints' Day?

Ninety-two percent of the Waray General Population (GP) go to the gravesite of their ancestors on All Saints' Day, as opposed to only thirty-one percent of the Assemblies of God (AG) respondents who do so. There is clearly a huge difference in the attitudes of the two populations on this question. As with some of the other subjects discussed in this research, the important issue is why they do or do not go.

TABLE 7.1
Reasons for Going to the Gravesite on All Saint's Day

	GP (426 Resp.)		AG (152 Resp.)	
	Yes	No	Yes	No
1. To leave an offering for the spirits of the dead?	404 (94.8%)	21 (5.2%)	72 (47.4%)	80 (52.6%)
2. To clean the gravesite?	410 (96.1%)	16 (3.9%)	118 (77.6%)	34 (22.4%)
3. To have a family reunion?	390 (90.8%)	36 (9.52%)	101 (66.3%)	51 (33.7%)

Cleaning the gravesite and having a family reunion are not theologically significant, except for those who include dead relatives as part of the reunion. These common reunions on All Saint's Day clearly indicate the cultural value of the family among the Waray.

The major theological issue here is related to leaving offerings for the spirits of the dead. The Waray, like most lowland Filipinos, believe that the spirits of the dead return to their graves on this day and expect to be fed. If they are not, they may put a curse on the living members of the family. Nearly all of the GP bring an offering for the dead, which is not surprising. But that almost fifty percent of the Assemblies of God people who go to the gravesite also do so is cause for concern. This may be explained when the differences between the members and the adherents are examined later. When given the opportunity of offer additional reasons for going to the gravesite, some in the GP, along with a few of the AG, said they went to pray, offer candles, or to fulfill a cultural tradition.

Only twenty-three percent of the members of the AG go to the gravesite on All Saints' Day as opposed to eighty percent of the adherents who do so. Again, the reason why they go or do not go is the most relevant question.

TABLE 7.2
AG Reasons for Going to the Gravesite on All Saints' Day

	Members (98 Resp.)		Adherents (54 Resp.)	
	Yes	No	Yes	No
1. To leave an offering for the spirits of the dead?	23 (21.1%)	75 (78.9%)	49 (90.7%)	5 (9.3%)
2. To clean the gravesite?	68 (69.4%)	30 (30.6%)	50 (92.6%)	4 (7.4%)
3. To have a family reunion?	59 (60.2%)	29 (39.8%)	42 (77.8%)	12 (22.2%)

While the differences in the data were significant on all three reasons given, only the responses to the first reason are theologically relevant. The vast majority of adherents continue to leave offerings for the dead at the gravesite, apparently still believing that the dead can return. While this also is a problem for some in the members' category, the numbers are comparatively small, revealing a large difference between these two groups.

The difference between the two groups in question one is not surprising, given the trend in the adherents to respond more like the GP than the AG. It is, however, a bit unusual that there would be substantial differences in the scores on the second and third questions. Here, the members show less of an inclination to clean their relative's graves or have a family reunion on this day. It may be that members do not want to be associated with the idea of spirits returning to the gravesite or perhaps, being freed from the need to appease the ancestors, members may be less inclined to spend the money and time for reunions and grave cleaning.

But eight percent of the GP and sixty-nine percent of the AG respondents do not go to the gravesite. Again, the reasons for not going are important.

TABLE 7.3
Reasons for Not Going to the Gravesite on All Saints' Day

	GP (36 Resp.)		AG (339 Resp.)	
	Yes	No	Yes	No
1. No time?	10 (28.6%)	25 (71.4%)	92 (27.4%)	244 (72.6%)
2. Cannot go home to attend?	6 (17.1%)	29 (82.9%)	32 (9.5%)	304 (90.5%)
3. Leaving an offering for the dead is idolatrous?	11 (30.6%)	25 (69.4%)	265 (78.6%)	72 (21.4%)

There is no critical biblical issue at stake in questions one and two. The significant issue here is in question three, leaving an offering for the dead. That thirty point six percent of the General Population sees it as idolatrous is not particularly high because most people in this group do not go to the gravesite. Sixty-nine percent of the Waray and twenty-one percent of the Assemblies of God say that not going to the gravesite is unrelated to the belief that that practice is idolatrous. The Assemblies of God people, however, do make a statement about their convictions in that more than three quarters of those interviewed said that leaving an offering for the dead was biblically wrong.

The AG gave some additional answers. Eighty of them added that going to the gravesite is useless because the dead are already dead. This gives a strong indication that they believe that the dead are no longer able to return and to influence the living, therefore, appeasing them with an offering is unnecessary, as suggested earlier. Thirty-seven also said that they do not go because they know the truth now that they are born again, underscoring a belief that the dead are no longer a problem for them.

What Does the Bible Say?

Death is the main theological issue related to going to the gravesite. The idea of the dead returning is quite common among the Waray, and there are a number of superstitions, rites, and taboos to deal with this. But because the belief that the spirits of the dead return to the gravesite on All Saints' Day is by far the most popular, it is the focus here.

Ninety-two point four percent of the GP go to the gravesite on All Saints' Day and nearly all of them leave an offering for the dead (see Table 7.1 on page 108). By contrast, among the sixty-nine percent of the AG population that does not go, the overwhelming majority do not go because they believe that leaving an offering for the dead is idolatrous. The differences between them and the GP are near polar opposites. Why is this so?

Leonardo Mercado (1992:21) states well the Waray belief about the dead returning:

> The cemetery is often a place where the living visit the dead and ask for their advice. The scene of All Saints' Day and All Soul's Day on November 1 and 2 show that the dead are not entirely gone. People believe that the departed have a new form of existence. Together they still form one extended family.

Among those who go (see Table 7.1), the vast majority of the GP and almost half of the AG do so to leave an offering for the dead in the belief that the dead have the power to bless or curse their descendents. They can cause crop failure, illness, and other kinds of misfortune. The Waray also believe that the dead can influence the living, implying that they have at least some knowledge of what is happening in the lives of their descendents, as well as having at least some power to influence their future. Among the AG population, most of those who leave offerings for the dead are adherents (see Tables 7.1. and 7.2 on pages 108 and 109). This means that they have not yet come to maturity in Christ in this area of their lives.

When given the opportunity to give additional answers to the question about going to the gravesite, forty-six of the GP respondents and six of the AG said that they go there to pray. Many of them specifically said that they pray to the spirits of the dead, which is a form of necromancy.

What does the Bible say about praying to the spirits of the dead? In Deuteronomy 18:9-12, where Moses taught the children of Israel how to live in the Promised Land, the practice of consulting the dead is specifically condemned along with other forms of witchcraft and sorcery. In 1 Samuel 28:3-20, God was displeased when Saul asked a medium to bring up Samuel from the dead. Isaiah 8:19-20 is clear that those who lead others in praying to the dead are not doing so on God's behalf. In answering the question as to why necromancy is condemned, the answer is implied in 1 Samuel 28:16-18. Saul practiced necromancy because he had nowhere else to turn; he had been rejected by God because of his disobedience in failing to destroy the Amalakites. In his case, necromancy was simply the ultimate end of a life of rebellion.

In 1 Samuel 15, where Samuel confronted Saul with his disobedience in failing to destroy all of the Amalakites, he warned him that God viewed rebellion and divination as the same thing. The heart of the sin of divination here is that God was not at the center of what Saul was trying to do. This is why most forms of divination are forbidden by God.

But the core issue in this question is centered on whether the dead can return to earth. Any biblical teaching among the Waray on the theology of death must deal with this issue. Hebrews 9:27 teaches that after death comes the judgment of God, suggesting that returning to earth apart from accompanying Christ at his second coming is impossible. The apostle Paul accents this thought when he writes that to be absent from the body is to be present with the Lord (2 Corinthians 5:8).

The Bible has a lot to say about death and the afterlife. Physical death is perceived to be the end of earthly existence (Myers 1979:898). The ancient Hebrews, like many of the ancient near Eastern peoples, pictured the abode of the dead as cut off from earthly life (Myers 1979:900). One of the most common terms of the Old Testament abode of the dead is *Sheol*, which is "frequently personified with gaping jaws and an insatiable throat (Proverbs 1:12; Isaiah 5:14; Habakkuk 2:5)" (Myers 1979:900). Allen Myers correctly states that the future of the unrighteous and righteous are more clearly distinguished in the New Testament (Matthew 7:13ff; 11:23; Philippians 1:23). The righteous will go to Heaven and the unrighteous to Hell, which will ultimately be swallowed up in the Lake of Fire. Generally speaking, the Bible does not speak of the dead returning to earth nor of the dead being able to communicate with or impact the living.

There are, however, some striking exceptions. In the Old Testament story of Saul and the witch at Endor (1 Samuel 28), the witch screams when she sees Samuel coming up from the grave. The Bible does not say why she was so shocked, but the text is clear that it was indeed Samuel who arose. In this case, he came to deliver a message from God that Saul and his sons would die the next day.

In the New Testament, Jesus raised numerous people from the dead in order to demonstrate his power over death. Perhaps the most poignant of these was the raising of Lazarus (John 11:38-44), no doubt prefiguring his own death and resurrection about a week later.

Another example of the dead reappearing occurred during the Transfiguration of Christ in Matthew 17:1-13 and Luke 9:28-36, where Moses and Elijah appeared and spoke with Jesus, discussing Jesus' future suffering on the cross. Obviously, the most outstanding example of the dead coming back to life is the resurrection of Christ himself.

In at least two cases, however, the purpose of God is not explained. 2 Kings 13:20-21, gives an interesting anecdote about a group of Israelites who were burying a man in the same cave where the prophet

Elisha was buried. As they were burying the man, they saw a band of marauding Moabites, got scared, threw the dead man inside the cave, and ran away. The corpse accidentally touched the bones of Elisha, and the dead man instantly came back to life with no explanation given. The other case occurred at Jesus' resurrection. Many previously dead righteous people came out of their tombs, went into Jerusalem and revealed themselves to people (Matthew 27:51-53). Perhaps Matthew mentions it here to emphasize Christ's power over the grave, but again, no explanation is given.

In summary it can be said that the dead cannot return on their own accord and that they have no power to bless or curse the living. They are cut off from the living. However, God in his own wisdom may occasionally cause the dead to be brought back to life in order to accomplish his own purposes.

In comparing what the Bible teaches to what the Waray believe, there are some striking differences. One, when the dead returned in the Bible, with the possible exception of Samuel, they always returned *in* the flesh, not simply in spirit. Second, they returned with a purpose from God to accomplish, and were not free to follow their own whims. Third, in the Bible, the dead who returned had no power over the living, to bless or to curse. Fourth, in the Scriptures the dead return only rarely, not *en masse* on All Saints' Day.

Do You Attend the Town or Barrio Fiesta?

Almost seventy nine percent of the GP attend the fiesta. This seems a bit low given the pervasive social nature of the event in their communities. Some clues as to why this is so will be uncovered when the reasons why people do not go are reviewed. Only thirty-two percent, or nearly one-third, of the AG population attend, suggesting that there may be some disagreement in the church ranks on this issue as going is normally frowned upon by church leadership. Why this number is so high will be examined later.

As was true with the previous question regarding going to the cemetery on All Saints' Day, the real issues lie in why they do or do not go to the fiesta.

TABLE 7.4
Reasons for Going to the Fiesta

	GP (363 Resp.)		AG (156 Resp.)	
	Yes	No	Yes	No
1. To eat good food?	288 (79.6%)	74 (20.4%)	82 (52.6%)	74 (47.4%)
2. To attend the special mass?	338 (93.4%)	24 (6.6%)	43 (27.3%)	113 (72.4%)
3. To attend the dance?	116 (32.1%)	245 (66.9%)	30 (19.3%)	126 (80.7%)
4. To participate in the religious procession?	324 (89.3%)	39 (10.7%)	32 (20.6%)	123 (79.4%)
5. To have a family reunion?	330 (91.7%)	30 (8.5%)	120 (77.4%)	35 (22.6%)

There was a significant difference between the GP and the AG on all questions. But do the differences matter? Going to the fiesta to eat good food is not contrary to Scripture. The same is true with going for the sake of a family reunion. The overwhelming majority of both sample populations indicated that this is one of the reasons that they go.

The responses of the Assemblies of God people who go to the fiesta that they feel free to attend to eat and have family reunions. Only about one third of the GP respondents attend the dance, suggesting that they do not feel that this is the main event of the fiesta. Since the Assemblies of God has generally not approved of dancing, considering it worldly, the fact that some attend may reflect disagreement with church teaching.

The major theological issue here is the special masses and the processions, both of which are done in honor of the patron saint of the town, *barangay* or barrio. The processions are colorful, with crosses in the front and the images of the saint or saints towards the rear.

There is a tremendous difference between the GP and the AG regarding these two practices. Nearly all of the GP attend the special masses, while, by comparison, only about one fourth of the Assemblies of God people do so. A somewhat lower percentage of each group participates in the processions, but the difference is still large. This indicates how pervasive the worship of the saints is in Waray society, a fact that is consistent throughout this study. While the numbers of the AG people who attend the masses and processions are much higher than one would have hoped, these figures are drawn only from the portion of the AG population that goes to the fiesta. If one compares, for example, that out of the 493 total respondents in the Assemblies of God only forty-three go to a special mass, the overall percentage is small. The same holds true for those who attend the procession.

Some respondents gave additional reasons for going to the fiesta such as to visit friends, go for a stroll or see the cockfights.

Of the 425 members who responded to this question, only twenty seven point one percent said that they attend the annual fiesta while sixty-one percent of the adherents also go. Here's why:

TABLE 7.5
AG Reasons for Going to the Fiesta

	Members (115 Resp.)		Adherents (41 Resp.)	
	Yes	No	Yes	No
1. To eat good food?	52 (45.2%)	63 (54.8%)	30 (73.1%)	11 (26.9%)
2. To attend special mass?	12 (10.4%)	103 (89.6%)	31 (75.6%)	10 (24.4%)
3. To attend the dance?	14 (12.2%)	101 (87.8%)	16 (39%)	25 (61%)
4. To participate in the religious procession?	6 (5.3%)	108 (94.7%)	26 (63.4%)	15 (36.6%)
5. To have a family reunion?	85 (83.3%)	29 (16.7%)	35 (85.4%)	6 (14.6%)

In questions one and five, no biblical issues are at stake. Question three reveals that the adherents have a greater tendency to attend the dance than the members. The important issues here are in questions two and four, with the results revealing a significant divergence of opinion. The adherents show a much greater tendency to participate in these events than the members, suggesting that they have not yet had a paradigm shift in their thinking on these issues.

Those Who Don't Go to the Fiesta

Twenty-one percent of the GP and sixty-eight percent of the AG said they do not go to the fiesta.

TABLE 7.6
Reasons for Not Going to the Fiesta

	GP (97 Resp.)		AG (336 Resp.)	
	Yes	No	Yes	No
1. I don't want to go.	48 (49.5%)	49 (50.5%)	177 (52.3%)	159 (47.7%)
2. I want to go but don't have time.	27 (28.2%)	69 (71.8%)	32 (9.5%)	305 (90.5%)
3. My pastor says its wrong	17 (18.1%)	77 (81.9%)	182 (54.5%)	152 (45.5%)

Only a relatively small percentage of the GP say that they do not go because their pastor says its wrong. If this were to be compared with the total number of GP, 462, only about four percent object to the fiesta on moral or spiritual grounds. Perhaps one could argue that because most of the Waray are Catholic and they have priests, not pastors and that therefore the nomenclature here confuses the issue. This is a possibility but because the Roman Catholic Church fully endorses the fiesta and encourages its people to participate, this is not a major point. For the Assemblies of God people, this is one of the most important reasons why they do not go. There may be a correlation between this and the first answer, people not wanting to go because their pastor says it's wrong. When they were asked to give additional reasons why they didn't go to the fiesta, many responded that they knew it was idolatrous, suggesting that it was not only their pastor's conviction, but also their own.

In all three questions, the AG people register a fairly high negative response. This may suggest that in many cases, the real reason as to why they do attend the fiesta may not have been mentioned here. Twenty-five AG respondents also indicated that they don't go because the fiesta is dedicated to the saints and another seventeen said they do not go because they are now followers of Christ and know the truth.

TABLE 7.7
Reasons Why AG People Do Not Go to the Fiesta

	Members (310 Resp.)		Adherents (26 Resp.)	
	Yes	No	Yes	No
1. I don't want to go?	165 (53.2%)	155 (46.8%)	12 (46.2%)	14 (53.8%)
2. I want to go but don't have the time?	25 (8.1%)	285 (91.9%)	19 (73.1%)	7 (26.9%)
3. My pastor says it's wrong?	175 (56.8%)	133 (43.2%)	7 (26.9%)	19 (73.1%)

The only issue here relevant to a contextual theology is question three. Many AG pastors believe that going to the fiesta is wrong because of the connotation of idolatry. That only about fifty-seven percent of the members don't go because their pastor says it is wrong may indicate some differences of opinion within the AG on this issue. Here, however, the adherents were much more likely to say that this was not the reason that they avoided the fiesta.

What Does the Bible Say?

The biblical issue regarding the town fiesta is idolatry because the fiesta or at least the religious parts of it, is dedicated to the saint of the area in which it is being held. Two main parts of the fiesta are dedicated to the saint, the special mass or masses that are said in their honor, and the religious procession, which can also held at other times. The purpose of the fiesta is twofold: to give thanks to the saint for what he or she is perceived to have done for the people such as sending rain and protecting them from evil and to appeal to the saint to continue helping the people.

The substantial differences in the scores between the GP and the AG (see Table 7.5 on page 117) suggest a strong difference in values.

Almost all of the General Population and about a quarter of the AG attend the special masses in honor of the patron saint, a slightly lesser percentage on each side go to participate in the religious processions. The GP then value activities that honor the saints.

But is this idolatry? The Catholic Bishops' Conference of the Philippines (CBCP) (1997:249-250) has written:

> Catholic Filipinos are attracted much to images and statues of Christ, Mary and [the] patron Saints. These images can offer genuine aid in their worship of Christ and veneration of God's blessed, Mary and their patron saints. But in the Philippines today, many who misunderstand the nature and function of venerating sacred images, reject this practice as idolatry. Against such attacks the Church firmly insists on the valuable help such images can offer for authentic Christian prayer. Nevertheless, the church is equally insistent on the proper use of such images, avoiding any and all appearances of making the images into idols, or treating them as endowed with some magical powers (cf. CCC 2132). This need for caution is confirmed by today's 'image industry' which graphically illustrates how manipulative and deceitful human images can become, even holy images.

Thus, the Catholic church denies that using images in the religious processions and honoring the Virgin or the saints in the mass is idolatrous. While the Church does admit that these have become idolatrous in some instances, the difference between a legitimate use of the images and an inappropriate use is not clear in this text. Also, there appears to be a difference between what the church actually teaches and what the people believe, as many are convinced that images possess magical powers.

Jaime Belita (1991:97) helps explain why the issue of images is important to Filipinos:

> This is no place to argue as to possible 'idolatries' for God alone knows what is in the heart of the worshipping believer. In

entering practices of popular religiosity to help understand Christ's person and work, it is with the assumption that visual images and artistic works have a role to play in faith and worship; that symbols and rituals, in fact, are valid, if not indispensable, not only in religious but also in socio-psychological activities, even the most secular ones. The use of images and symbols surrounding them are more helpful for self-understanding among the illiterate and the popular imagination, for that matter.

Belita justifies the use of images on the basis of Filipino culture, not the Holy Scriptures. What he is saying is that the images are nothing more than a visual aid to assist people in worshiping the Lord and that religious images are no different that secular images in their intent and usage. But Belita's simple dismissal of the issue of idolatry here by saying that God alone knows the heart of the believer, while true, does not obviate the need to consider whether the use of images is right or wrong according to the Bible.

Idolatry can be defined as giving to someone else the honor, worship and veneration that belongs to God alone. The Scriptures abound with references to idolatry, indicating that God takes the subject seriously (i.e. Leviticus 19:4; 26:1; Deuteronomy 29:17; 2 Chronicles. 15:8; Galatians 5:20).

Exodus 20:1-6 is the most succinct passage in the Bible about idolatry and is even more powerful when understood in light of its historical context. Exodus 20 forms part of a body of teaching given by God through Moses as the Israelites were camped around Mount Sinai only a few months after God had gloriously delivered them at the Red Sea. The exodus had been preceded by the ten plagues, which clearly reveal God's attitude towards idolatry. The Egyptians were a polytheistic people, with Pharaoh himself at the head of a pantheon of gods, a fact well known to the Israelites.

In Exodus 12:12, God makes clear that the intent of the plagues, especially the killing of the firstborn, was an act of judgment on the gods of Egypt. What happened in the plagues was nothing less than a systematic assault on the Egyptian pantheon. Gailyn Van Rheenen (1991:110) describes the situation well:

> The account in Exodus indicates that the deliverance was a contest between Yahweh, the God of Israel, and the god-king of the Egyptians (and the sun-god who stood behind him). God sent the plagues to force pharaoh [sic] to acknowledge that 'no one is like the LORD our God' (8:10; 9:14 NASB). The Egyptian magicians recognized the plagues to be the 'finger of God' (8:19 NASB), an admission of Yahweh's superiority. Even pharaoh [sic] confessed Yahweh's superiority: 'I have sinned this time; the LORD is the righteous one, and I and my people are the wicked ones' (9:27 NASB).

In missiological terms, God was challenging the religious worldview assumptions of both the Egyptians and Israelites, who had watched this outpouring of the wrath of God on their captors. For the first time, this Israelite generation saw their God in action in a power encounter without parallel in the Old Testament. Certainly God also intended to communicate his displeasure of idolatry to the Egyptians, but I believe that his primary intent was to reveal himself to his own chosen people. While Israel did forget God's attitude toward idolatry, they never forgot the events that took place in the Exodus. This is the historical context in which Exodus 20 must be understood.

In looking then at Exodus 20:1-6 more closely, the issue of allegiance forms part of the context in verses four and five. Here, after stating that the children of Israel were not to bow down to other gods or serve them, it states that God is a jealous God. Of what is God jealous? The conclusion is inescapable that God is jealous that his people have might give allegiance to other gods, an allegiance that is rightfully his alone because it was he who had delivered them from slavery in Egypt.

But the Israelites failed to keep God's command. Exodus 32 records the first incidence of idolatry in the history of the nation of Israel. While Moses was with God up on Mount Sinai, the children of Israel waited for his return down below. When Moses did not come down right away, the people became impatient and demanded that Aaron give them gods to worship. The people's felt need was for something they could see.

So Aaron made an image of a calf and proclaimed it as the image of the God who had delivered them, in direct contradiction of the commandments his own brother was then receiving from God up on the mountain. They celebrated the advent of this new "god" with a fiesta, sacrificing, and revelry, much like the Canaanites whose land they would eventually invade, until Moses came down from the mountain. Moses' reaction, breaking the tablets that contained the Law forbidding idolatry (Exodus 20:1-17), was symbolic of what the people were doing by worshiping the image. He had broken the Law of God written on tablets, and they had broken the Law of God that was written on their hearts.

Another incidence of idolatry occurred when the Israel became divided into two kingdoms. Jeroboam, the first king of the northern tribes, wanted to ensure the people's loyalty (I Kings 12:25-33). He knew, however, that if they continually went to Jerusalem to worship as God had commanded, they might be enticed to reunite with the southern kingdom. To counteract this, he had two calves made, which he said were representations of the one, true God, intentionally deceiving the people. Abraham Terian (1982:795) suggests that Jeroboam's golden calves may have some resemblance to Aaron's calf. One was placed at a shrine in Dan, at the northern boundary of his new kingdom and the other was placed in Bethel, at the southern end. He appointed a priesthood and offered sacrifices. A prophet of the Lord came to the shrine at Bethel and prophesied against it (1 Kings 13:1-4), but every king that followed Jeroboam was condemned by God for not taking the shrines away, thus following in Jeroboam's sin.

There is more to idolatry than images, but the question remains as to why the use of images is so emphatically and expressly condemned in the Bible J. Rodman Williams (1996:1:49) attempts to explain:

> God as the living God, first, is One who stands in opposition to all idolatry and graven images. Idols of any kind, because they are inanimate—"they cannot speak, they have to be carried, for they cannot walk" (Jeremiah 10:5)—stand over against the living God. "But the LORD is the true God; he is the living God and the everlasting King" (Jeremiah 10:10). Thus to worship an idol is to worship a dead object and to profane the living God. Indeed, any graven image (Exod. 20:4), even if it be an attempt to portray the true God, is also an abomination because the living God cannot be reduced to a lifeless image of Himself.

Simply stated, images fail to represent the character of God. But, according to Williams here, there is more. Images, which cannot see, hear, touch, feel or smell, insult the character of the living God himself.

About 100 years after Jeroboam, Ahab, the king of Israel and his Phoenician wife, Jezebel, established the cult of Baalism in the northern kingdom (Huey 196:246). Baal was believed to be the god of agriculture, controlling the crops, the rain and anything else related to planting and harvesting. This attracted the Israelites, who were agriculturists, and they began offering sacrifices to Baal in order to be assured of a good harvest and without pestilence or famine. Again, as is normal in animistic practices, there was no thought of worshiping Baal in adoration. They simply appeased him in order to get what they wanted.

In this religious context, then, it is easy to see why the story of Elijah and the prophets of Baal gets full coverage in I Kings 17 and 18. The point of God withholding the rain (1 Kings 17:1) was to demonstrate that he is the true God, not Baal. The power encounter to come was designed to show that Baal was a fraud. No doubt there were many appeals to Baal for rain during the three and a half years of drought and the situation became quite desperate (1 Kings 18:2), but God sent no rain. God's curse on his own people for their disobedience is consistent with the terms of the covenant laid out in Deuteronomy 28:15-19. When the people finally came to repentance after a dramatic power encounter on the top of Mount Carmel and recognized again who was the true God, he removed the curse and sent rain.

The Israelites were also greatly tempted to worship Asherah, the goddess of fertility who was symbolized by placing sacred poles in sacred groves of trees. Since barrenness was seen as a curse, many succumbed to the temptation. They also fell prey to worshiping the gods of other nations around them, such as Chemosh, the god of the Moabities, and Moloch, the god of the Ammonites to whom children were offered as sacrifices. In the end, God brought judgment upon his own chosen people.

Before moving on to what the New Testament says about idolatry, a few issues need to be clarified. The Bible is clear that images themselves are impotent. In riveting prose, both Isaiah and Jeremiah detest those who would make idols because the idol itself is a powerless deception (Isaiah 44:9-20; Jeremiah 10:1-5). However, as Moses mentions in Deuteronomy 32:16-17, and as Paul makes abundantly clear in I Corinthians 8 and 10, idolatry is inspired by demons. On the basis of Exodus 20:1-4, the main issue here, as far as mankind's relationship with God is concerned, is allegiance. Idol worship, then, is inspired by the powers of darkness in order to draw the allegiance of people away from the one true God.

The New Testament does not have as much to say about idolatry as the Old because its emphasis on Jesus Christ and the Kingdom of God (Matthew 10:7), but idolatry was still a challenge to the church as the good news spread among the Gentiles. Since the first followers of Jesus were nearly all Jewish, it may be safe to assume that idolatry was not an issue among them. However, as the Christian faith spread beyond the borders of Palestine, it made contact with various pagan religions.

Mystery religions, such as those encountered by Paul in Ephesus and elsewhere, were common and, in time, the cult of worshiping the Roman emperor would also become a serious challenge to the new faith. For those who would receive Christ and leave their other religions to become a Christian, the issue of allegiance to the one, true God, who disallowed images even of himself, would have become abundantly clear.

Three specific texts, Romans 1:18-32, 1 Corinthians 8 and 1 Corinthians 10, will be dealt with here to understand what the New Testament says about the nature of idolatry and how Christians living in idolatrous societies should respond to it.

In Romans 1:18-32, Paul goes back into the early religious history of mankind. Verses 18-20 speak of what is known as "general revelation," the knowledge of God being known through observing what he has created. Verse 19 is clear that mankind understood who God was because he had plainly revealed himself to them, a statement with which even the Stoic philosophers of the day would have agreed (Keener 1993:416). Because God's revelation of his own power was so clear in his creation, no one had an excuse. Craig Keener (1993:416) notes that the truth suppressed in verse 18 is the truth about the character of God. The suppression is done through idolatry which distorts God's true character. Understanding verses 21-22 is pivotal to understanding idolatry in the New Testament. Although mankind clearly understood who God was, they intentionally and unequivocally rejected him. Rather than worship the one true, omnipotent God, they preferred to worship what he created. In the words of verse 25, "they exchanged the truth of God for a lie." These few words in and of themselves succinctly expose the heart of idolatry. According to John Murray (1965:42), Paul's intent here is to contrast the glory of God with the foolishness of worshiping what was created. In worshiping creation rather than the Creator, the heart of man became degraded.

God's reaction was to give mankind what they wanted (v. 26). One might ask what idolatry has to do with the sexual immorality described so graphically by Paul here. There are two correlations evident in this passage. Both idolatry and sexual immorality involve rejecting God's moral standards of behavior as embodied in the Ten Commandments. They are also selfish acts, doing what is wanted by the individual and giving no thought to God. Keener (1993:416) insightfully adds that one's view of God influences the way one treats others sexually. Not only is sexual perversion a result of idolatry, so are the other kinds of sins listed in verses 28-32.

The Corinthian passages were written to people who had undoubtedly come out of a pagan background. Corinth, located on an isthmus in southern Greece, was a seafaring community at a crossroads for people from all over the Roman world. Keener (1993:451) notes that the many foreign merchants may have contributed to the presence of foreign religions. The temple of Aphrodite, the goddess of love, with all of its temple prostitutes and notorious Empire wide reputation, did nothing to improve the moral values of the city.

Keener (1993:452) also says that roles and places in society were determined by social status, which would have placed some believers in social situations where meat offered to idols was also offered to them. While the Jews in cities such as Corinth would have likely had their own market and, therefore, one would know that the meat sold there did not come from the temples of idols, someone eating at the house of an unbelieving friend would not have known the source of the meat. This is the issue Paul focuses on in chapters eight and ten.

In 8:1, the phrase "now about" occurs several times in this epistle, suggesting that Paul was responding to questions from the Corinthian believers about various issues. Most scholars think that the believers had written a letter to Paul, which no longer exists. In this case, then, Paul was responding to issues that they themselves had raised.

The foundation of his argument in both passages is that believers are to walk in love, giving more heed to the feelings of others than their own opinions. This suggests that there may have been disagreement among the believers on the issue of eating meat offered to idols. The second premise of his argument, taken from the Old Testament (cf. Isaiah 44:9-11; Jeremiah 10:5), is that idols are nothing in and of themselves, and that this is true because there is only one God.

The phrase in verse 7 "but not everyone knows this," however, indicates a transition in his argument and most probably refers to new believers, who may still be tempted to go back to a lifestyle of idolatry. If one exercised their spiritual liberty by eating in a temple of idols, knowing that the idol in itself is nothing, others who see them may be drawn back into a sinful lifestyle (vv. 9-13). In this case, the law of loving one's brother in Christ takes precedence over exercising one's freedom.

While eating meat dedicated to idols may be harmless and while the idols themselves are not true gods (1 Corinthians 10:19), it does not follow that participation in pagan sacrifices is appropriate (1 Corinthians 10:20). Alluding to Deuteronomy 32:17, Paul says that sacrificing to idols is in fact sacrificing to demons. Verse 21 suggests that the issue of allegiance may also be in view here as one cannot have fellowship with demons and also with the Lord. Wilhelm Mundle agrees (1971:286) when he says that "fellowship with Christ, which Christians enjoy in the Lord's Supper, excludes communion with these powers. Christians should not challenge the Lord. If they do, they will bring down his judgment on them" (1 Colossians 10:7-10, 14-22). I Corinthians 10:22 is no doubt a reference to Exodus 20:1-6, which states that God is jealous of those that worship other gods because the allegiance of those for whom Christ died is rightfully his.

In I Corinthians 10:27-31, Paul gives some practical advice. When one is dining in the home of an unbeliever, don't ask about where the meat was obtained. This will avoid any issue of conscience. But if it is discovered that the meat was sacrificed to idols, one should abstain.

Leon Morris (1979:778) interprets this that if one were to eat the meat in a situation like this, one would be condoning idolatry. Therefore, for the sake of the purity of the gospel, it would be better to risk offending the host than to give the impression that idol worship is sanctioned by God.

The application for the Waray is simple. While the food sold at the town fiesta is not dedicated to idols, one's presence at the fiesta might become a stumbling block to a weaker brother. If this is true, other believers must then avoid the fiesta. And they must do it with a servant's heart, not an arrogant attitude that considers them to be more spiritual than those who might stumble. I Corinthians 10, where Paul expressly condemns any and all actual participation in pagan sacrifices, finds a resonant cord with many in the AG population, who agree that participation in the parts of the fiesta specifically dedicated to the saint is wrong.

Apart from the issue of allegiance, there are other reasons why idolatry is wrong. First, it is wrong because there is no other God, as Isaiah 45:22 makes clear. Any other entity that is worshiped as a false god, and anyone else claiming to be God is an imposter. But there is another reason that is just as critical.

F. B. Huey (1976:248) gives several other reasons as to why idolatry is wrong:

> One person may look upon it as a representation and void of value or power in itself, but another may regard it as the abode of the god and fraught with power, and therefore he will worship the image. A visible representation of the deity tends to restrict a person's concept of God, for he will base his concept of God, consciously or unconsciously, upon the image or picture. Finally, man becomes like that which he worships (Hosea 9:10).

The first reason given by Huey relates well in the Waray context. As mentioned elsewhere in this chapter, Catholic scholars hold that the images are nothing more than visual aids to worship but, a vast difference exits between what the church actually teaches and what the average Waray believes. The line, therefore, between visual aids and actual worship is thin or nonexistent.

The truth expressed in the second reason given by Huey is, no doubt, one of the major reasons that God prohibits idolatry. As no image can accurately describe him, any image of God would not be an accurate representation of him. Huey's final statement that idolatry ultimately debases man as well (Hosea 9:10), finds further expression in Romans 1:24.

The question may be raised as to why idolatry looks attractive. One reason is that it is selfish. The Israelites worshiped or appeased other gods to give them whatever they wanted. Donald Stamps (1992:394) also notes that the pagan religions did not require the kind of obedience that the God of Israel required and their moral standards were much lower.

With the exception of the Virgin Mary, there is no love for the object of veneration in view here. It is worship in the sense of appeasement, not adoration, in order to manipulate the supernatural being to do the will of the worshiper. Stamps (1992:394) is correct that one cannot truly understand the lure of idolatry unless one understands its true nature. While the idol itself is nothing, it is used by demons to draw away one's allegiance from God. Interpreting this passage in the Philippine context, to honor the saints for sending rain, healing their bodies, or protecting the community from disaster, as many of them are reputed to do, is to give the saints honor that rightfully belongs to God. In this sense, there is no difference between the images that God rails against in Exodus 20 and those of the patron saints that are honored in the town fiestas and religious processions in the modern Philippines.

Chapter 8

QUESTIONS ABOUT SICKNESS AND HEALING

In this chapter we will explore what the Waray believe regarding both the causes of sickness and the sources of healing. Studying both will give deeper insights into their worldview as well as help identify the theological issues that need to be taught for life-transformation at the worldview level and for a full experience of the gift of salvation with healing.

Causes of Sickness According to the Waray

TABLE 8.1
Beliefs Regarding Causes of Sickness

	GP (462 Resp.)		AG (492 Resp.)	
	Yes	No	Yes	No
1. Germs or unsanitary conditions?	433 (94.3%)	26 (5.8%)	466 (94.7%)	26 (5.3%)
2. Spirits?	336 (73.7%)	120 (26.3%)	407 (82.9%)	84 (17.1%)
3. God?	137 (29.8%)	323 (70.2%)	64 (13.1%)	426 (86.9%)
4. Sorcerers?	346 (76.%)	109 (26.%)	361 (73.5%)	130 (26.5%)
5. Witchdoctors?	218 (47.2%)	244 (52.8%)	302 (61.5%)	189 (38.5%)

There was no significant difference between the two populations on the first question regarding germs as a source of sickness. No theological issue is at stake here, but it does reflect a high acceptance of the premise of Western medicine regarding the transmission of disease.

There was, however, a significant difference between the two groups as to whether spirits can cause sickness. By comparison, the AG people were much more likely to ascribe the cause of sickness to spirits. Why this is so is somewhat speculative. Perhaps being a Christian has heightened their view of the spirit world. Both sample populations, however, exhibited beliefs that the attitude the spirits can cause sickness, an attitude that has enormous implications for divine healing and presenting the gospel with attendant signs and wonders.

The difference between the two groups was even more significant when they were asked if God can cause sickness. Both groups showed reluctance to blame God. Just under one third of the GP and thirteen percent of the AG said that he could do so. Yet the question remains as to why the GP scored higher in this category.

The difference in the data on the question regarding the sorcerers was not significant. Both populations show a fairly high degree of conviction that sorcerers can cause sickness. Since Waray society generally thinks of them as evil, it is not surprising that both groups share the same viewpoint.

There is a substantial difference in the data regarding whether witchdoctors can cause sickness. Here, the AG group scores much higher. While those in the GP do acknowledge that witchdoctors can cause sickness, they more closely reflect the general attitude that these people are benevolent. The higher score of the AG can be explained as part of the already mentioned paradigm shift that has taken place in their thinking and their value system.

When given the opportunity to offer additional answers, respondents in both groups listed lack of faith, pollution, vices, not eating properly, and overwork as other causes of sickness. But what about the differences between the AG members and adherents?

TABLE 8.2
AG Beliefs Regarding Causes of Sickness

	Members (425 Resp.)		Adherents (67 Resp.)	
	Yes	No	Yes	No
1. Germs or unsanitary conditions?	404 (95%)	21 (5%)	62 (92.5%)	5 (7.5%)
2. Spirits?	361 (85.1%)	63 (14.9%)	46 (68.7%)	21 (31.3%)
3. God?	54 (12.7%)	370 (87.3%)	10 (15.1%)	56 (84.8%)
4. Sorcerers?	314 (73.9%)	111 (26.1%)	47 (71.2%)	19 (28.8%)
5. Witchdoctors?	277 (65.2%)	148 (34.8%)	25 (37.9%)	41 (62.1%)

In question one regarding germs, the percentages are similar but no biblical issue is at stake. There were significant differences on questions two and five, whether the spirits and witchdoctors cause sickness, but not on three and four, whether God and sorcerers can do the same. The members showed a greater tendency to admit that spirits can cause sickness. Why this is so is not immediately clear. Perhaps the members felt more comfortable in sharing their real feelings on this issue, although the adherents do not appear to have been shy with their opinions on other subjects.

The members were also more prone to say that witchdoctors cause sickness. In coming to know Jesus Christ, many of the members have discovered that the witchdoctors do not work for God, as many of them claim. As a result, they have a lower opinion of them than would those adherents who are just coming to know Christ.

What Does the Bible Say?

Table 8.1 on page 131 reveals a strong conviction by both the GP and the AG that sicknesses can have both natural and supernatural origins, the differences in their scores being only a matter of degree. Novilla (1971:58) notes that belief in the supernatural origin of sickness is particularly true in the rural areas. Yet a significant minority believes that both God and the witchdoctors are capable of causing sickness. Whether or not this is a real or perceived contradiction in biblical terms remains to be seen. The AG respondents reflect a more consistent viewpoint, the majority indicating that spirits, witchdoctors and sorcerers are all capable of inflicting sickness, with a small minority believing that God also does so.

Studying the causes of sickness and suffering is closely related to the concept of God's blessing and cursing. The Bible clearly teaches that sickness entered the world because of sin and, therefore, it can be truly said that sin is the root cause of sickness (Genesis 3:9-19). Satan induced Eve to sin. This leads Gordon Wright (1984:35) to suggest that Satan is the first cause of all sin and suffering.

Since most of the practices of the witchdoctors and sorcerers are explicitly forbidden by God, the Bible clearly places their activities in the realm of evil (Malachi 3:5-6; Acts 13:6ff; 16:16ff; Revelation 21:8; 22:15). Therefore, a biblical comparison will be done between sicknesses caused by the forces of evil and sicknesses that God may inflict or allow, if it can be established that God or Satan and his minions cause sickness. Not only will the causes of sickness and suffering be studied, but also any purposes or goals in allowing sickness that might be found in the Bible.

Table 8.2 on page 133 indicates that the Waray believe that sickness can simply come from natural causes. While the Bible doesn't have a lot to say about this directly, the idea of preventing sickness may be behind many of the sanitation and ceremonial laws in the book of Leviticus.

The Bible has much to say, however, regarding whether sickness can be caused by spirits. In the opening chapters of Job, it becomes clear that Job's suffering is directly caused by Satan, yet only with God's permission and within the limits that God established (cf. 1:12; 2:6). While God allowed Satan to afflict Job, the direct causality of his illness came from Satan.

While Job's afflictions were primarily physical, there is also a case of mental illness. In I Samuel 16:14 the Bible says that an evil spirit from the Lord tormented Saul. Since there is no evidence of actual demon possession, it may be true that, as Wilkinson (1998:50-51) suggests, that his true illness may have been a bi-polar disorder. But causality is the issue here. In this case, the text is clear that it was brought on by a demon sent by God. One must agree with David Edwards (1979:61) that, while evil spirits were regarded as malicious authors of physical maladies, they were not, in a strictly dualistic fashion, thought to act in complete independence; rather, they had a certain place assigned to them in the divine providence. In other words, no matter what Satan and his hordes desire to do, they are not independent of God. All of the reasons why God allows suffering go well beyond the scope of this study as does the related question as to whether God is morally responsible for evil.

Isaiah 45:7 specifically says that God creates calamity. Edwards (1979:61) notes that when the ancient Hebrews were afflicted, they had no problem seeing it as coming from God and did not doubt his sovereignty. Why God afflicted men was a question they often asked. In the following references, the Bible specifically states that God himself sent the sickness. In Genesis 12:10-20, God cursed Pharaoh because he took Abram's wife. The intent of the affliction was to get Pharaoh's attention regarding his sin. Since Pharaoh took Sarai without knowing that she was really Abram's wife, it may be that the sicknesses were not intended to be punitive. In Exodus 10-12, God specifically sent the Ten Plagues to execute judgment on gods of Egypt (Exodus 12:12). By contrast, God promised the children of Israel that he would not inflict these diseases upon them if they walked in obedience to him (Exodus 15:26).

In Leviticus 26:16, 25 and Deuteronomy 28:21, God specifically promised that he would curse the Israelites with diseases if they did not obey the covenant. Exodus 32:35 and Numbers 25:1-9 are ample testimony that when they failed to keep the covenant, God did not fail to bring down his promised judgment. Israel was judged for grumbling and discontent against God and Moses (Numbers. 11:33; 16:41-50). In 1 Samuel 5:6-12, the Philistines were struck with illness wherever they brought the Ark of God. In 2 Kings 6:18, soldiers invading Israel were temporarily blinded by God.

God also judged individuals. In Numbers 12:10, Miriam became a leper for a week for speaking out against Moses. The ten spies who did not believe in God's power to give them the promised land died of a plague at the hand of the Lord (Numbers 14:37). One must agree with Michael Brown's (1995:135) statement, however, that not all sickness is a result of personal sin.

In other passages, God is not mentioned directly, but his power is obviously involved in executing the affliction mentioned. Angels blinded the men of Sodom who sought homosexual relations with them (Genesis 19:11). Jeroboam's hand was withered (1 Kings 13:4), Gehazi became a leper (2 Kings 5:27) and Nebuchadnezzar was smitten with mental illness (Daniel 4:29-32).

In trying to assess why God sent or at least allowed sickness, several suggestions may be made. In many of the cases above, God punished a nation or an individual because of sin. In other cases, such as Pharaoh (Genesis 10:12-20) or the Philistines mentioned above, God apparently afflicted them to warn them. Being animists who believed that sickness can be a curse from the spirit world, God knew that afflicting them would certainly get their attention.

Not all cases, however, fit these categories. In 2 Samuel 24:10-17, seventy thousand people died because of David's sin of numbering the people of Israel. Of the three options that God had given him here, being afflicted with a plague was likely the least punitive in David's mind, as he had great confidence in the mercy of God. There are other cases in the Old Testament where the cause of illness is not mentioned (i.e. 2 Kings 4:18-20). When sickness was brought on by divine wrath, the only remedy was repentance (Brown 1995:103-104).

Sicknesses can come from natural causes, Romans 8:18-22 reveals that the created order was impacted by the fall of man into sin. Wright (1984:25-26) interprets this passage to mean that germs and other microorganisms causing sickness became a threat because of the fall since there was no sickness before then.

Demonic possession is generally regarded as a form of illness. In this case, however, it is a sickness that involves direct contact with Satan and his hordes. In a number of places in the gospels, demon possessed people were also deaf, dumb or both (i.e. Mark 9:17, 25). When Jesus cast out the spirits, they could then both hear and speak.

In Luke 13:11-13, Luke, a medical doctor, records Jesus' healing of a woman who had been crippled or bound by a spirit, directly associating sickness with demons although, as Wilkinson (1998:141) states, it was not actual demon possession. In a summary statement in Acts 10:38, Luke states that Jesus went about healing those who were "under the power of the devil," suggesting that he believed that the devil can oppress people through sickness.

In the case of the man born blind (John 9:1-41), the disciples assumed divine causality here in judging either his or his parent's sin. Jesus empathetically denies that this is true in this case. He simply states that the man was allowed to be sick in order that the glory of God might be seen through healing him. John did not ask whether God actually caused the sickness, but it must be stated that God allowed it. Richard Lee (2000:46-47) writes that this miracle resulted in increased faith in the disciples and the man himself came to know Christ.

In Luke 1:1-45 Zacharias was struck dumb because of his unbelief in the power of God to give him and his wife a son. That his dumbness was punitive is obvious from verse 20, but it also served to send a clear message to others that something divine was happening. In the end, God was honored by what he said when he was able to speak again (Luke. 1:67-79).

In the book of Acts there are several instances of sickness or even death that are ascribed to God. God killed Ananias and Sapphira for lying to the Holy Spirit (Acts 5:1-11). Understandably, this display of God's holiness brought great fear to the church, causing the members to reverence the Lord in a much greater way. In Acts 9:1-18, God struck Saul of Tarsus with blindness. There is no reason to think that the blindness would have only been temporary had God not healed him. In this case the purpose of God was two-fold. First, God planned for Saul, who became Paul, to experience salvation through Jesus Christ. Second, God planned to call him as a missionary to the Gentiles. In Acts 13:6-12, a sorcerer tried to stop the Roman proconsul from listening to and believing what Paul and Barnabas were sharing about faith in Christ and God struck him also with temporary blindness. As a result he, no doubt, was humiliated before the proconsul, who probably lost confidence in his supernatural abilities. This demonstration of the power of God convinced the proconsul to believe in Christ.

In the New Testament cases reviewed here, God struck people with illness in order that he might be glorified through them. He was glorified through revealing his power to judge in the case of Ananias and Sapphira, and through revealing his power to heal in the case of the man born blind. Both the man born blind and the Roman proconsul came to Christ as a result of demonstrations of the power of God. In all of the cases mentioned here, God revealed his purpose in allowing or causing sickness and suffering.

The Waray view that germs, spirits, witch doctors and sorcerers (the latter two acting as agents of the devil) can bring sickness is essentially correct according to the Bible. The vast majority of the GP, however, would not see the witchdoctors as servants of the evil one.

Both sample populations failed to measure up to the biblical standard in their view of God's ability and willingness to inflict people with sickness in order to achieve his purposes in their lives or in society as a whole. This suggests that the Waray might not see the character of God's justice. The purpose of God in inflicting sickness, in many cases, was to either warn people that what they were doing was wrong, or to execute judgment for their sin. As far as the AG population is concerned, it may be a lack of teaching or the fact that this aspect of God's character is not popular and makes people uncomfortable.

Sources of Healing According to the Waray

TABLE 8.3
Beliefs About Who Can Heal People

	GP (460 Resp.)		AG (492 Resp.)	
	Yes	No	Yes	No
1. A witchdoctor?	403 (87.6%)	57 (12.4%)	127 (25.9%)	363 (74.1%)
2. God or Jesus?	448 (97.4%)	12 (2.6%)	490 (99.6%)	2 (.4%)
3. A sorcerer?	141 (30.9%)	316 (69.1%)	45 (9.2%)	445 (90.8%)
4. A medical doctor?	453 (98.7%)	6 (1.3%)	473 (96.5%)	17 (3.5%)
5. The Santo Niño?	383 (83.4%)	76 (16.6%)	41 42(8.4%)	450 (91.6%)
6. Other Saints?	380 (83%)	78 (17%)	41 (8.3%)	451 (91.7%)
7. The Virgin Mary?	382 (83.4%)	76 (16.6%)	51 (10.4%)	441 (89.6%)

The vast majority of the GP believe that witchdoctors can bring healing, while only about twenty-five percent of the AG people agree. In Waray society, people who say that they believe that the witchdoctor can bring healing normally would go to one if they become ill. This may explain the relatively low score regarding the witchdoctors' ability to heal in the Assemblies of God population. However, this may not be entirely true with the AG community, where there may be some that believe that witchdoctors can heal, even though they themselves do not go to them. This will be looked at again in chapter ten where the same AG respondents were asked if they actually go to witchdoctors now that they are Christians.

Regarding God or Jesus, as expected, the results were closer than some of the other scores. Why the AG group showed a higher tendency to believe in God for healing than the GP is not immediately clear, given that, in chapter six, both groups showed an equal propensity for prayer to God in times of need. The important issue here is that both groups exhibit strong confidence in the power of God to heal.

Neither group revealed a strong belief that sorcerers can heal, although the GP scored much higher on this issue than the AG. The high negative scores of both populations here reflect the general Waray belief that while sorcerers can heal, especially in revoking the effects of curses that they have made, they are better known as society's troublemakers. Both groups reveal a strong trust in doctors, the General Population giving slightly more trust to doctors than do the AG. But having a high trust in the medical profession does not mean that the Waray readily go to them when they are sick, because doctors are more expensive.

About eighty-three percent of the GP believe that healing can come from the Virgin Mary, Santo Niño or other saints, and a small percentage of the AG people agreed with them. The same respondents who believe that the Virgin can heal, also believe that the Santo Niño and the other saints can do the same. Those that reject one also tend to reject the others, meaning that they do not see much difference between these spirit beings, but believe that as long as one gets healed, the identity of the supernatural entity is irrelevant. The witchdoctor's role is to harness these spiritual forces in order to gain healing for mankind, and the average Waray believes that the spirit's power ultimately comes from God.

Again, the difference in thinking between the GP and the AG is apparent in that the overwhelming majority of the AG population does not believe in healing from these other spirit beings. There is a consistency between the AG responses to this question, and their responses as to whom they pray in times of trouble in chapter six. About ninety percent of the AG population prays to God alone, firmly believing in his power to heal.

We will now take a closer look at the AG population's responses, especially at the contrasts between the answers of the members and adherents.

TABLE 8.4
AG Beliefs About Who can Heal People

	Members (425 Resp.)		Adherents (67 Resp.)	
	Yes	No	Yes	No
1. A witchdoctor?	80 (18.9%)	343 (81.1%)	47 (70.1%)	20 (29.9%)
2. God or Jesus?	424 (99.8%)	1 (.2%)	66 (98.5%)	1 (1.5%)
3. A sorcerer?	38 (9%)	386 (91%)	7 (10.6%)	59 (89.4%)
4. A medical doctor?	408 (96.5%)	15 (3.5%)	65 (97%)	2 (3%)
5. The Santo Niño?	9 (2.1%)	415 (97.9%)	32 (47.8%)	35 (52.2%)
6. Other saints?	7 (1.6%)	418 (98.4%)	34 (50.7%)	33 (49.3%)
7. The Virgin Mary?	13 (3.6%)	412 (96.4%)	38 (56.7%)	29 (43.3%)

Regarding question two, the percentages reflect similar attitudes AG members and adherents about praying to God for healing. In question four, there is no biblical issue involved so the inability to analyze more closely is not relevant. There were significant differences between the GP and the AG on question one regarding witchdoctors.

In question one, the members showed a lesser tendency to believe in the witchdoctor's ability to heal than did the adherents. This is consistent with the members and adherents' responses to whether or not the witchdoctors could cause sickness in that both groups indicate negative attitudes towards witchdoctors.

The greatest divergence of opinion comes in the responses to questions five, six and seven. On these issues, these two groups are poles apart, the adherents showing a much greater tendency to believe in someone other that God for healing. Within each group, however, the scores are remarkably similar indicating, for example, that the members have much the same attitude toward the Santo Niño's ability to heal as the Virgin Mary's or the other saints ability to heal. The same could be said regarding the raw scores of the adherents, implying that those who believe that the Virgin can heal also believe that the Santo Niño and the other saints can heal as well.

What Does the Bible Say?

Here, our focus will be limited to whether God or other spiritual forces may bring healing, and what the purposes of healing might be. Table 8.3 on page 139 indicates that the GP believe that healing can come from several supernatural sources, a typical animistic approach. On the other hand, the AG respondents overwhelming reject healing from any other supernatural source other than God.

From a biblical standpoint, a response to the GP on this question is closely linked to the issue of idolatry in chapter seven. If the idols prayed to by the Waray are not real, then it stands to reason that they also cannot heal. But the issue isn't quite that simple. That witchdoctors can heal, directly or indirectly, through the power of spirits is well known among the Waray. If their power is not from God, what is its source? In response to this issue, Galvez-Tan, a Filipino medical doctor and researcher among the Waray, states (1977:19) that about seventy percent of the illnesses treated by witchdoctors are illnesses from which people would normally eventually recover from without treatment. Also, some of the herbs used in treating sicknesses may have real medicinal properties that actually bring relief. But all of this does not answer the question in every case. By what power, then, does the witchdoctor heal? Can Mary, the saints or the spirits heal? It was noted earlier that demons are behind idol worship. Since the witch doctors are not serving the one true God, the spirits with which they are in contact are demons also. Part of answering the question of healing then is asking whether or not healing can come from the powers of darkness. If so, what might be the devil's motive for healing?

In Exodus 7:8-24, the magicians in Pharaoh's court did imitate two of the miracles that were performed by God through Moses and Aaron. Gordon Wright (1984:19) is correct in saying that while the miracles performed by the magicians were inferior to that of Moses and Aaron, they were, nevertheless, real miracles. In Deuteronomy 13:1-3, Moses warns against following false prophets who are capable of doing signs and wonders. While healing is not mentioned here, the ability of the powers of darkness to do miracles, albeit with the intent to deceive, is real. Colin Brown (1986:371) also adds that the term "signs and wonders" in this passage does not necessarily mean violations of the natural order, which is the standard definition of a miracle. If false prophets can do signs and wonders, then they also may be able to heal.

In Matthew 12:22-29, when the Pharisees accused Christ of casting out demons by the power of the prince of demons, Jesus did not deny the existence of Satanic power (Wright 1984:19). In verse 27 Jesus mentions the Jewish exorcists, freely stating that they cast out demons, although he does not reveal the source of their power.

In 2 Thessalonians 2:9-12 (cf. Revelation 16:13-14), Paul ascribes to the anti-Christ the power to do miracles, and that God allows those miracles to deceive those who have intentionally rejected the truth. Wright (1984:19) regards these miracles and signs and wonders as counterfeit, and he is right in the sense that they are not performed by God. However, they are still miracles.

In looking at these verses, the possibility that the powers of darkness can heal cannot be denied. In spite of this, however, there is no clear and irrefutable evidence that the powers of darkness can bring healing. The question then as to how spiritists can bring healing through their secret arts or how people can be healed by praying to an idol cannot be completely answered, and more illumination by the Holy Spirit is needed here.

Does God Heal? In the Old Testament, the issue of healing begins with Exodus 15:26, where God states that Israel will be spared the plagues visited upon the Egyptians if they will obey him. Michael Brown (1995:237) notes that the Mesopotamian region at the time was full of healing deities. He adds (1995:238):

> In the ancient Near Eastern world, what distinguished the belief in Yahweh as Healer from the other purported healing deities was the OT's staunch monotheism. . . . emphasizing clearly that it was one God who both smote and healed, and he was anything but cavalier in his actions. Worship of any other so called god was not only forbidden, it was absolutely unnecessary. The Lord alone was sufficient. In fact, when Moses declared to his people that the Lord would be Israel's Healer, he was not primarily turning his people away from human, medical help. . . . Rather he was cautioning them against looking to any other god for aid.

Whether or not the other deities could heal is not the issue here. The point is that God alone is sufficient to meet every need.

Only a few healings are mentioned in the Old Testament. Naaman, the Syrian military commander, was healed of leprosy (2 Kings 5:3-14). Hezekiah was healed of a boil (2 Kings 20:1-7). On three occasions the dead were raised 1 Kings 17:19-23, 2 Kings 4:18-37, and 2 Kings 13:21.

By contrast, the New Testament records many healings. The ministry of Jesus was replete with them. Roland Harrison (1982:646) notes that the diseases healed by Jesus were common in first century Israel. While this may be true, Michael Brown (1995:227) adds that Jesus' healing ministry was closely linked to the ministry of healing people from illnesses related to Satanic power, including deliverance from demons (i.e. Luke. 13:10-17). Colin Brown (1986:373) notes that the gospels do not sharply differentiate between Jesus' miracles of healing, demonic deliverance or miracles of nature.

But why did Jesus heal? Colin Brown (1986:373) notes that the "The miracles of Jesus cannot, however, be detached from his teaching, the course of his ministry or indeed the reason why the Pharisees and others sought to kill Him." Michael Brown (1995:225) adds that this validation regarding Jesus' miraculous ministry:

> Was in keeping with the pattern of miraculous confirmation found throughout the OT. In spite of the possibility of counterfeit signs, wonders, and miracles. . . . God backed up his servants with demonstrations of his power, thus attesting to the truthfulness of their missions and calling (e.g., Ex 4:1-9, 29-31; Nu 16:28-35; I Ki 18:36-39), and at the same time, triumphing over idolatrous and counterfeit powers (e.g., Ex. 8:16-19).

Following this line of thinking, miracles are used to attest to the reality that God is the all-powerful, one and only God that he claims to be.

In Matthew 10:5-7, healing is one of the signs mentioned as heralding the arrival of the Kingdom of God. In the broader context of this passage, Matthew 9:35-10:42, Jesus is among the masses, preaching the Good News of the Kingdom, repentance and deliverance from sin, and authenticating the message by healing the sick. At the same time, Jesus called his disciples together and empowered them also to cast out demons and heal the sick (Matthew 10:1-5). This delegated power or authority was given in order to announce the arrival of the Kingdom of God. Therefore, one of the purposes of divine healing is to reveal the power of God over sin and its results, thus reversing the curse of the Fall (Genesis 3).

The connection between sin and sickness is as well established in the New Testament as in the Old. Michael Brown (1995:212-213) notes that the same Greek word commonly used for salvation in the New Testament can also refer to deliverance from demons or healing from sickness. In Matthew 9:1-8, Jesus demonstrated his authority to forgive sin when he healed a paralytic. Agreeing with his critics that only God can forgive sin, he was then used this miracle to authenticate his claim to deity. One can agree with Arsenio and Edith Dominguez (1989:32) that the miracles of Christ can only "find their meaning in light of Jesus' messiahship."

The purpose of healing may also be seen in an eschatological sense. Michael Brown (1995:218) notes that "the ministry of Jesus and his followers was a ministry of restoration and emancipation, to culminate ultimately in the glorious liberty of the children of God (Romans 8:19-23; 2 Corinthians 5:1-5; Revelation 21:4; see Acts 3:19-21)." In divine healing, there is a sense of hope that the day will come when sin and sickness be no more.

The impartation of authority to the apostles in Matthew 10:1 has never been revoked. Healing is part of the ongoing ministry of the church. Stamps (1991:1420) notes that:

> After Pentecost, the early church carried on Jesus' healing ministry as part of preaching the gospel (Acts 3:1-10; 4:30; 5:16; 8:7; 9:34; 14:8-10; 19:11-12; cf. Mk 16:18; 1Co 12:9, 28, 30; Jas 5:14-16). The NT records three ways that God's healing power

and faith were imparted through the church: (a) the laying on of hands (Mk 16:15-18; Ac 9:17), (b) confession of known sin, followed by anointing the sick with oil and the prayer of faith (Jas 5:14-16), and (c) spiritual gifts of healings given to the church (1Co 12:9).

If Jesus Christ is the same yesterday, today and forever, then there is every reason to believe that God still heals today.

In summarizing the issue of healing, the question of where spiritists get their healing power is not clear in the Scriptures. Therefore, a conclusive answer cannot be given. But because the GP are likely to give their allegiance to whoever brings healing, it can be said that allegiance must be given to God, whether or not he chooses to heal them. The Waray's high view of God's ability to heal is well justified by the Scriptures and suggests that the Waray, both believers and unbelievers, are open to the healing power of God. For the GP, this belief in God's power to heal stems from their worldview. For the AG, belief in God's healing comes not only from their worldview but also their understanding of the Scriptures.

Why they believe that God heals was not put to the Waray, but this is important to this study. If the Good News is going to be proclaimed among the Waray, it must be with accompanying signs and wonders so that they will understand that the Kingdom of God is among them. Since the Waray are open to supernatural healing, the teaching that God's power to heal is available to all who give their allegiance to him alone is good news indeed!

Chapter 9

QUESTIONS ABOUT EVIL SPIRITS

The Waray belief in the existence of the spirit world has already been amply demonstrated. But not all beings in their spirit world are benevolent. Fear of malevolent spirits and the felt need for protection is a driving force behind many Waray religious practices. The three questions presented in this chapter reveal these beliefs and practices: (1) How do you protect yourself from evil spirits? (2) Can people become controlled by evil spirits? (3) If they are controlled, are the results of possession good or bad? When we examine what the Bible says about these subjects, we find both agreement and disagreement between the two groups studied. However, we also find that the vast majority of AG responses more closely mirror the biblical truth about demons than do those of the GP.

How Do You Protect Yourself From Evil Spirits?

TABLE 9.1
Beliefs on How to Protect Oneself From Evil Spirits

	GP (463 Resp.)		AG (492 Resp.)	
	Yes	No	Yes	No
1. Getting an *orasyon* or amulet from the witch-doctor or priest?	197 (43.2%)	259 (56.8%)	27 (5.5%)	465 (94.5%)
2. Going to the pastor for prayer?	306 (66.8%)	152 (33.2%)	449 (91.3%)	43 (8.7%)
3. Praying directly to God in the name of Jesus for protection?	440 (95%)	23 (5%)	489 (99.4%)	3 (.6%)

Comparing the GP and AG strategies for protection from evil spirits revealed significant differences. The percentage in the GP who get an *orasyon* (a special class of amulets) for protection is surprisingly low. Nevertheless, it does reflect that a substantial part of the Waray fear malevolent spirits and try to protect themselves by wearing an amulet, generally around their neck or waist. However, the majority that does not wear amulets may find other ways to deal with their fear. The same could be said for the AG population which also feels no need of amulets. Where do they go for protection?

Nearly sixty-seven percent of the GP say they go to a pastor for prayer. This poses some problems for getting a clear answer regarding how the GP protects itself from evil spirits. One, the vast majority of the people are Roman Catholic and have priests, not pastors. Thus, there may be some bias in the question that would lower the percentage that said yes, although how much this may have impacted their response cannot be measured. First, given that most of the Waray are only nominally Catholic, the percentage that say they go to a pastor for prayer may actually be a little high. Second, and more serious, is that many would go to the priest to have their amulet blessed, thus possibly confusing the issues. At any rate, the data does suggest that the Waray see the pastor/priest as someone who can intercede for them. On this point, the AG people agree, with the vast majority going to their pastor for prayer.

Regarding prayer to God in the name of Jesus, the sample populations were much closer, although the difference between them still significant. But does this difference matter? It appears that both groups highly regard the power of God as a protection from demonic powers, a fact that is highly relevant for Pentecostal witness.

What is notable here is that while ninety-five percent of the GP believe that the name of Jesus is a powerful protection from evil spirits, more than forty percent wear amulets, as opposed to only five point five percent of the AG population who do the same.

TABLE 9.2
AG Peoples' Beliefs on How to be Protected From Evil Spirits

	Members (425 Resp.)		Adherents (67 Resp.)	
	Yes	No	Yes	No
1. Getting an *orasyon* or amulet from the witch-doctor or priest?	7 (1.6%)	418 (98.4%)	20 (29.9%)	47 (70.1%)
2. Going to the pastor for prayer?	401 (94.4%)	24 (5.6%)	48 (71.6%)	19 (28.4%)
3. Praying directly to God in the name of Jesus for protection?	424 (99.8%)	1 (.2%)	65 (97%)	2 (3%)

It is interesting to note that scores for the adherents fall between the GP and AG members in response to this question. In question two, the reason a lesser percentage of adherents might rely on the prayers of a pastor may be that they are new believers or possibly even not yet born again. Therefore, they lack the long term relationship with their pastor that the members have.

Question one reveals that the adherents have a greater tendency to put their trust in *orasyons* or amulets, while the members mostly reject them. While question three reveals a high degree of trust in God in both groups, this must be understood in light of question one, suggesting that a strong minority of the adherents do not trust in God alone. The data fits what might be expected from a segment of the church population that is comprised of new believers and people who are in the process of coming to Christ.

What Does the Bible Say?

Protection from evil spirits is the theological issue behind the eighth question in the survey regarding how the Waray protect themselves from evil spirits. In Table 9.1 on page 149, forty-three percent of the GP indicated that their protection comes from the amulets that they get from witchdoctors or priests, sixty-six point eight percent go to a pastor for prayer, and ninety-five percent of them also pray to God in the name of Jesus for protection. In their perception, going to a pastor and going to God may be the same or at least similar, as the pastor or priest is believed to have connections with God. In many cases it would appear that many pray to both God and wear amulets, apparently not seeing any contradiction between the two.

The AG respondents feel a stronger need to go to their pastor for prayer than do the GP and highly agreed on the need and opportunity to ask for protection from God. However, there is a sharp disagreement over the need to use amulets, with only five point five percent of the AG population saying that they wear them. It would seem that there is a correlation between their felt need to go to God or their pastor and the lack of need to turn to amulets.

The Scriptures never questions the reality of evil spirits nor of the need of human beings to be protected from them. Therefore, the felt need of the Waray for protection is understandable. But how should that protection be secured and what qualifications might there be from the one giving protection? The Old Testament refers to the devil in I Chronicles 21:1, Job 1 and 2, Psalms 109:6 (KJV) and Zechariah 3:1-2, and gives a clear allusion to him in Genesis 3:1-19. Demons are referred to in Leviticus 17:7 (KJV); Deuteronomy 32:17; 2 Chronicles 11:15 (KJV); and Psalms 106:37. In the Leviticus and 2 Chronicles passages, where the King James uses the term devils, the NIV uses the words "goat idols." There is no contradiction here. Harrison (1976:96) notes that goat worship was common in Lower (northern) Egypt and involved a number of depraved rituals. Since the Israelites came out of the same part of Egypt they would likely have been familiar with these practices. All of the references to demons here are in the context of sacrificing to them. While the idea of fearing demons is not specifically mentioned in any of these verses, it would have been a strong motivation for appeasing them with offerings.

There is also the issue of false gods, who are really a front for demons (Deuteronomy 32:17). While this has been covered adequately elsewhere, I mention it again here because the fear of these other gods tempted the Israelites to sacrifice to them. They feared that if they fail to offer appeasing sacrifices, the gods would execute their wrath. Thus, they would feel at least some need for protection.

When all of the evidence for demons in the Old Testament is considered, one must note the lack of a comprehensive demonology. Harrison (1976:98) suggests that the subject of demons and demonology wasn't important to the Old Testament writers. Aune (1979b:919-920) agrees, stating that while the existence of demons was never in question, "the ancient Israelite notion of Yahweh's sovereignty did not encourage nor necessitate the development of religious thought in this area." This is also understandable because the focus of the Bible is on the Kingdom of God, not the dominion of darkness.

How does one protect himself from demons? Amulets, charms, talismans, and fetishes are not appropriate because they are designed to manipulate spiritual forces that are not oriented towards God. For the same reason, they are ultimately not effective. But does God provide protection from demonic forces?

While the Old Testament does not appear to have a lot to say on this particular issue, it does address the matter. Psalm 91 may well be the most descriptive passage in the Bible regarding God's protection against demonic powers. Michael Brown (1995:152) says that Psalm 91:3-6 "may contain the fullest list of demonic powers – under various descriptive figures of speech in the OT." Some commentators do not mention the occult overtones of this passage, but the reference to demonic powers cannot be discounted here. In reference to verses 5-6, Marvin Tate says (1990:455):

> The language is metaphorical and designed to encompass a whole range of potentially lethal happenings. Nevertheless, there is no reason to doubt that the content of the psalm reflects a

thought world in which the presence of demons, demonical possession, and malignant spirits and powers was considered commonplace. The text of the psalm reflects a sense of synergistic inner connection between ordinary life and the sinister powers of the occult. The demons and powers were especially manifest during epidemics and unexpected physical attacks, along with other varied catastrophes which threaten human existence.

The context of the animistic and polytheistic cultures of the peoples that surrounded Israel and impacted them greatly suggests that Tate's understanding of this passage is correct. The Israelites would likely have taken these verses to refer to the powers of darkness and would have found great comfort in God's protection.

Psalm 91:1-4 speaks clearly of God being a refuge for those who trust in him. Verse 4 has the imagery of a mother hen or numerous other kinds of birds, protecting their young from the predators of nature. To a pastoral people like the ancient Hebrews, the imagery would have been a powerful statement of God's loving protection of his own. In the second part of the verse, like the walls that protected their cities, so God would protect them from the unseen but real forces of darkness.

Verse 13 also carries the idea of God's protection in an powerful manner, suggesting that those who trust in God will encounter and overcome the powers of darkness. Michael Brown (1995:152) notes:

> Of course, this verse was not literally intended, but that does not mean that the creatures spoken of were not perceived as real. Rather, they referred to malignant spiritual enemies who would be rendered powerless because of Yahweh's protection and angelic host (vv. 11-12).

Although these verses are clearly poetic and figurative, the message of believers trampling on the powers of darkness in God's name is clear.

Throughout the psalm there is another strong theme that must be taken into account. God does protect people, but only those who trust in him. "The shelter of the Most High" in verse one is only for those who choose to dwell there (cf. verse 9). The issue is one of allegiance. Only those who have given their allegiance to God can expect his protection. There is no protection promised for unbelievers.

In the New Testament, Aune (1979b:922) writes that "in continuity with intertestamental Judaism, Jesus and early Christians regarded demons as real and powerful adversaries of man. Harrison (1976:98-99) notes that in the New Testament, there is no significant difference in the terms demons, evil spirits and unclean spirits. Furthermore, fear of the demonic is part of the colorful animistic background of at least two of Paul's epistles, Ephesians and Colossians. Clinton Arnold (1992, 1996) has explained this background clearly in two of his books which will be quoted from fairly extensively in dealing with the twin issues of protection from demons and demon possession.

Referring to the situation at Colossae, Arnold (1996:135) notes that one of the most significant reasons for joining the pagan cults was to get immunity from evil powers. This assumes a widespread fear of them. Arnold (1996:197-198) also notes that folk issues were known among the Jews of Asia Minor. The Colossians belief in the reality of such powers is evident in Colossians 1:16; 2:8, 10, 15, 20, where the powers of darkness are identified in various terms. If these cults were strong in Colossae, it is reasonable to assume that some of the new Christians would have come out of these cults and would still have to deal with fear of the demonic. Arnold (1996:251) agrees: "The structured emphasis on the 'powers' as an elaboration of the invisible realm underlies our impression of the nature of the root problem facing the Colossian Christians—they continue to fear the realm of evil supernatural forces that bring harm."

Paul helps them deal with their fear by pointing them to Christ. In Colossians 1:16, Christ is portrayed as the creator of all, demonstrating that he is the most powerful of all. Arnold (1996:260) sees in this verse the freedom from the powers of darkness that believers find in their Lord. In Colossians 2:8-10, the issue of allegiance comes in again as Paul encourages his readers to trust in Christ, in whom the entire Godhead dwells in bodily form. In verse 10, the reference to power and authority is a reference to demonic powers. In referring to the Godhead here, he is making another claim to the deity of Christ and his omnipotence. He is saying that Christ is worthy of trust because his power is greater than all of the powers of darkness.

Colossians 2:15 powerfully states that he broke the power of the forces of darkness. The context here is the power of Christ over the power of sin, but the point is still the same. The mention of a public spectacle here is a reference to when the Caesars of Rome returned victoriously from battle, flaunting their power over their captives by parading them down the streets of Rome in public ridicule and humiliation. This, according to Paul, is precisely what Jesus did to the powers of darkness through the cross.

In Colossians 2:20, the powers of darkness are implied in the term "basic principles of this world." Arnold (1996:193) states that protection from demonic powers is implicit here, but that protection does not come automatically. Believers must choose to follow Christ and renounce the things of this world and, by proxy, the demonic powers that inspire them. The issue of allegiance is again evident here since renouncing the attitudes and philosophies of this world is part of demonstrating one's desire to wholeheartedly follow Jesus.

The biblical answer to getting protection from demons is to put one's trust in God, giving complete allegiance to him. This is possible because he is all powerful, able to protect all who call upon his name and is worthy of our trust and allegiance. AG respondents appear to understand this since the data in Table 9.1 on page 145 indicates only a few feel the need of amulets. Their two most numerous alternate responses also indicate their ability to give allegiance to their powerful

God: Twenty-seven said they just trust in God for protection, while twenty-four also said they claim the promises of the Word of God in this matter. Forty-three point two percent of GP (see Table 9.1 on page 149) put their trust in amulets. This suggests that their trust is not yet in God.

Can People Become Controlled by an Evil Spirit?

A logical conclusion of the Waray belief in the existence of evil spirits is that these evil spirits can possess humans. When asked if people could be controlled by an evil spirit, eighty-one percent of the GP responded affirmatively and eighty-five percent of the AG agreed with them. The difference between the two groups here was not significant. Clearly, the belief that demons can possess people is widespread among the Waray. But a further question must be asked. Do the Waray believe that the results of demon possession are good, bad or both?

TABLE 9.3
Perceived Results of Demon Possession

GP (369 Resp.)			AG (420 Resp.)		
Good	Bad	Both	Good	Bad	Both
7 (1.9%)	325 (88.1%)	37 (10%)	1 (.2%)	413 (98.6%)	5 (1.2%)

The overwhelming majority of the Waray in both groups believe that demon possession is bad, but the difference in percentages between the two groups here is statistically significant. The AG perceives demon possession as substantially worse than the GP. The two groups also differed in that the GP was more likely to see it as both good and bad. But in order to get a more complete picture of Waray beliefs on this subject, another question must be asked: Why?

The few who saw demon possession as good saw it as a benefit to humanity. Because of the Waray belief that spiritists possessed by demons can heal the sick and give guidance to people. But the overwhelming majority of both sample populations had a different view of demon possession. Those who saw it as both good and bad said it was good for the same reasons mentioned above and bad for the reasons mentioned below.

More than ninety-eight percent of the respondents in both groups said that demon possession is bad because demons control a person's body and because that possession causes them to lose consciousness and awareness of what goes on around them. Many respondents in both groups simply said that possession destroys the mental and physical capacities of the possessed. Many also said that the demon possessed walk and talk differently, describing such things as removing their clothes, talking incoherently with bad words, becoming stronger than normal, mental derangement, loss of consciousness and going crazy.

What is particularly important here is that the scores regarding the evilness of demon possession were virtually identical for both groups. The theological implications are enormous and will be explored later.

Turning to the AG opinion, over eighty percent of the members and adherents said that people can be demon possessed. Of the members who believe that people can become demon possessed, all but three said the result is bad. Among the adherents who agreed with the possibility of demon possession, most also said it was bad. Two said it was good and two more felt it was both.

What Does the Bible Say?

The vast majority of the Waray believe that people can become demon possessed. In this case, there was no significant statistical difference between the two sample populations, meaning that the attitudes of the GP and AG on this issue are virtually the same. If the results tabulated in Tables 9.1, 9.2 and 9.3 on pages 149, 151 and 157, respectively, are also considered, it can be said that the vast majority of the Waray believe that demon possession is bad, and it is bad because people lose control of their minds, bodies, and tend, at least temporarily, to lose their grip on reality.

For the purposes of this study, demon possession or control means to be physically entered by an evil spirit to the point where the demon controls all or some of the body's functions. Detailing the differences between oppression and possession as well as answering the issue as to whether or not Christians can be demon possessed are well beyond the scope of this study.

In the commenting on the general opinion of people in Palestine in the New Testament era, Harrison (1976:99) says that "possessing spirits were uniformly regarded as evil, and had to be expelled on all possible occasions, for they were allies of Satan and thus hostile to God and man alike." The gospel writers shared this view. This is in contrast to the Greek traditions of the day that held that demons might be considered both good and evil (Van Rheenen 1991:116). References to demon possessed people can be found in Matthew 15:22-28; 17:14-23; Mark 1:23-25; 5:1-20; Luke 11:14-28, and Acts 16:16-18.

In the Matthew 15:22-28 narrative, a Canaanite woman comes to Jesus, begging him to set her daughter free from demonic possession. When Jesus saw that the woman truly believed in his power to deliver, he set the girl free. In another case in Matthew 17:14-23, the demoniac clearly reveals irrational behavior, suggesting that epilepsy might have also been involved. There is no evidence of the boy's having faith in Jesus and, in Mark's account of the story (Mark 9:14-27), Jesus chides the boy's father for his lack of faith. Nevertheless, he still cast out the demon and healed the boy.

In Mark 1:23-25, the demon, using the man's voice and body, screams out in acknowledging who Jesus is. The spirit also caused the man to shake as he exited the man's body. In Mark 5:1-20, the man is evidently possessed by numerous demons, as they use the name "Legion," no doubt in reference to a Roman army legion that had as many as six thousand men. This does appear to be an intense case of possession as this man had also demonstrated anti-social behavior with his incredible strength, nudity, crying out and cutting himself with stones. With no apparent effort, Jesus expelled the demons, thereby releasing the man from the devil's grip. In Luke 11:14-28, Jesus drove out a mute demon. When the demon was gone, the man, who also had been mute, began to speak. This drew people's attention, and Jesus' skeptics raised the issue of his authority, claiming that it came from Satan because they doubted Christ's deity.

While more instances of demonic deliverance than this appear in the gospels, these accounts are representative of the deliverance ministry of Christ. Several things stand out in these narratives. On more than one occasion, the demons identified him as the Son of God Most High or gave some other ascription of his deity. They knew who he was. Also, in a number of the cases, the person involved was either physically or mentally dysfunctional because of the demons. The Waray reported the same thing. Finally, in each and every case, the absolute authority of Jesus Christ over demons is demonstrated by his ability to cast them out of people. When he spoke, Hell obeyed.

In contrast to the Old Testament, where references to demons are comparatively rare, the incidents where Jesus encountered demons were many. This frequency gives evidence to the adversarial role of demons in the Gospel writings (Van Rheenen 1991:114). The expelling of demons intentionally demonstrated the arrival of the Kingdom of God, where the Kingdom assaults and overcomes the powers of darkness (see Matthew 10). The message today is to proclaim that God's Kingdom has come to earth through Jesus Christ. The evidence of the in-breaking of the Kingdom today should be no different than in the time of Christ (Matthew 10:5). Through demonic deliverance, the Kingdom of God is not only announced in power, it also challenges existing worldviews and calls for allegiance to a new master, Jesus Christ, King of Kings and Lord of Lords (Van Rheenen 1991:125).

Demonic deliverance has continued through the ministry of the church. The experience of Paul and Silas in Philippi in Acts 16:16-21 is sufficient to make the point. A young lady was prophesying under the influence of demon powers. Like other cases in the New Testament she, too, through the powers of darkness, correctly identified the men, but in this case, a believer in Christ exercised his authority and cast out the demon in the name of Jesus.

According to Harrison (1976:99), "the concept of the 'power of the name' was widespread in antiquity and was based on the assumption that the 'name' was not only a personal designation but also represented an integral part of the personality of the bearer" (Harrison 1976:99). The superiority of the name of Jesus is well stated by Paul in Philippians 2:9-11.

This subject was already touched on in response to the question about protecting oneself from demons, because the supremacy of the power of God is directly linked to his ability and willingness to protect those who trust in him from hostile powers. However, this also becomes an issue in deliverance from demonic possession and is thus given further consideration here.

The authority of Jesus Christ over demons has already been demonstrated in the Gospels. Now it will be examined in light of Paul's letter to the Ephesians as this book, along with the epistle to the Colossians, provides the clearest teaching in the Pauline epistles on this issue. The supremacy of Christ over demonic powers is evident in Ephesians, especially when one understands the pagan religious background against which this epistle was written. Many of the terms Paul uses to describe the demon powers in this epistle were terms that were well understood by both the Jews and the Greeks in his day, indicating a common belief in the reality of the spirit world (Arnold 1992:69). Luke devoted much space to the miracles that took place through Paul's ministry in Ephesus in Acts 19:1-41. These miracles included the confrontation with the powers of darkness, the effort to co-opt that power by others, the considerable revival that took place and the riot that ensued. The emphasis on these miracles suggests that Luke well understood the power that the cult of Artemis had over the city and its influence over the minds of the people. Arnold (1992:168) explains the situation in first century Ephesus:

> Ephesus stands out as unique among Hellenistic cities because of the widespread and pervasive influence of her patron goddess, Artemis —a goddess of the underworld and intimately linked with magical practices... I have merely documented that magical practices *flourished* at Ephesus, and that underlying concern in connection with magic – fear of the demonic realm – was addressed as a primary theme in [the book of] Ephesians.

Arnold explains that the Ephesian magical practices connected to the cult of Artemis were motivated by fear of demons. Paul addressed these practices and the fear behind them which formerly prompted Ephesian believers to follow Artemis. This is important here because in addressing these issues, Paul demonstrates the power of God. Arnold (1992:138) explains:

> The *cosmic Christology* of Ephesians highlights the supremacy of the Lord Jesus Christ to 'all things' especially the malignant angelic 'powers.' The epistle stresses the close identification of the believer and this cosmic Christ, with the result that they now share in the power and authority of Christ over the hostile 'powers.' Their lives are no longer held in thrall by these forces.

Not only is Christ superior to the powers of darkness, but those who follow him also have this power over the devil and his demons. This supremacy of Christ is a recurrent theme throughout this epistle (Arnold 1992:129).

In 1:21, God's power is mentioned in direct relationship to the powers of darkness in verse 19 and that this power is at work in all believers. Here, Paul employs four different terms that in English are rendered, "incomparably great power," and "power" (Arnold 1992:73). It would seem that the apostle strains the limits of human language in his attempt to describe the greatness of God's power. In verse 20 (cf. Philippians 2:9-11), the greatest revelation of this power was at the cross where God crushed the powers of darkness once and for all. Arnold (1992:170) explains that while complete judgment upon the demonic powers will not be executed until the Second Coming of Christ, their powers have already been broken by his death, resurrection and exaltation. So believers need not fear them. For Ephesian believers this must have been exceedingly good news.

In 2:6, Paul restates the point made in 1:20-21 that believers are shown to have been raised up and seated with Christ. This is in contrast to their former position of being "dead in sin" (Ephesians. 2:1-2). Arnold (1992:158) suggests that this change of position now reflects a superior position of the believer in relationship to the powers of darkness.

In 3:14-16 (cf. Philippians 2:9-11) the matchless power of God is affirmed. All power in the universe is within God's providence. Nothing, not even the powers of darkness exist apart from him (Arnold 1992:58). In Ephesians 3:18, the concept of the power of God is expounded upon again. Here, the power of God is given to the believer to grasp the depth of the love of God extended to all who follow Christ. In other words, God does not use his power for his own selfish purposes, but for the benefit of all who trust in him. This power is sufficient to deliver all of the benefits that God desires to give, regardless of the strength of the powers of darkness that resist him (Arnold 1992:95-96).

The often quoted "armor of God" passage in 6:10-20, must be understood in light of this theme of the power of God in contrast to the powers of darkness (vv. 11-12). Arnold (1992:103) says that there are more references to the concept of power here than in any other passage ascribed to Paul in the New Testament. Perhaps this passage, more than any other, describes the human role in this conflict of the kingdoms as believers are challenged to arm themselves with spiritual weapons, both offensive and defensive, and enter the battle. This text is clear that the forces of darkness do assault believers (v. 11), although how this is done is not explained. The weapons, which are given by God to the believer, however, are powerful.

In summary, Paul thoroughly documents the greatness of the power of God in this epistle. His intent in doing so is to demonstrate that the trust of the Ephesian believers in God is well founded, and that their new faith is built solidly upon the rock of the character and power of God. Arnold (1992:73) notes that the magical practice of Ephesus greatly contrasts with faith in the living God whose power is supreme, sufficient, and personal.

Several comparisons can be made between what the Waray believe about evil spirits and what the Bible teaches about them. The Waray recognition of the reality of the dark powers is well justified by Scripture. The Waray also agree that spirits can possess people. The viewpoint of the GP and the AG on this issue is virtually identical which suggests the depth of this belief. The common Waray idea that demon possession is always bad is also well founded in the Bible. But the good news is that Jesus Christ is absolutely and completely Lord of the demonic realm and that his power to vanquish demonic principalities is absolute. This can and must be communicated to the Waray through teaching and through signs and wonders, especially healing the sick and casting out demons.

Chapter 10

HOW THE ASSEMBLIES OF GOD PEOPLE WERE TRANSFORMED BY THE GOSPEL

Any attempt at contextual theology must demonstrate how the people in a given culture are transformed by the gospel message and what aspects of that message impacted them the most. In this study, this information was gathered through a separate questionnaire designed for and administered only to AG members and adherents. The results will be analyzed here. The goal of this particular questionnaire was to determine how the gospel of Jesus Christ has changed their lives by looking at their attitudes on the following questions before they became followers of Jesus Christ and what they believe now. There is much evidence in the research data to suggest that a transformation has or is taking place among the AG respondents. But before this can be accomplished, a brief review of the doctrine upon which this transformation depends must be given.

The Doctrine of Salvation

The theological issue that underpins the entire second questionnaire is "What does it mean to be saved?" While the doctrine of salvation cannot be studied exhaustively here, this question can be adequately answered from two perspectives, position and allegiance.

When people come to Christ, a change of position has taken place. According to Colossians 1:13, God "has rescued us from the dominion of darkness and brought us into the kingdom of the Son he loves." When we were in the kingdom of darkness, we were slaves to sin and cut off from God (Ephesians. 2:1-10). But when Christ comes into the lives of people, he frees them from slavery to sin and brings them into his Kingdom to live under his Lordship. This is what the Bible calls salvation (cf. Colossians 1:13 and Ephesians. 2:4-6). We have already seen the victory that Christ bought for believers over the powers of darkness (Ephesians. 1:19-23). In the context of Ephesians 2:1-4, people are saved (or delivered) by grace from sin's enslavement . This means that while believers may still sin, they are no longer slaves to it.

While the actual transformation from the kingdom of darkness to the kingdom of light may take place in a moment, the outworking of that transformation is a process that happens over the course of a lifetime. This process of transformation appears to be what Paul had in mind in Philippians 2:12 where believers are challenged to "continue to work out your own salvation with fear and trembling," meaning that they are to continue to grow in their obedience to God. With this challenge to maturity comes the temptation to fall back to the old ways. Arnold (1992:123) addresses this temptation regarding spirit world issues:

> It cannot be assumed that the fears of these converts about the evil spiritual realm were immediately allayed by their new found faith. It would also be erroneous to assume that their conversion to Christianity would have brought about a complete forsaking of all their former means of protection from the hostile 'powers.' Even if many (or the majority) of Christians did totally turn aside from their former apotropaic practices, some at least would have faced a great temptation to combine their Christian faith with magical techniques.

In cases like these, teaching, patience and love are needed to bring new believers into their full inheritance as children of God.

But not only is salvation a change of position, it is also a fundamental change of allegiance. Jesus' message was "Repent, for the kingdom of heaven is near" (Matthew 3:2). A call to repent is a call to change one's actions and attitudes. In other words, it is a call to give one's allegiance to Christ above all else. A classic example of the change of allegiance that takes place within a believer is the apostle Paul in Acts 9. Before he met Christ, Paul was a Pharisee who thought that salvation was attained through the keeping of the Law and the progressive achievement of good works (Philippians 3:1-10). He was so zealous for the Law that he actively persecuted Christians, whom he considered to be blasphemers of the true God for proclaiming that Jesus Christ was the promised Messiah.

But his Damascus road experience changed everything (Acts 9:1-19). Now, rather than focus on the details of the Law, he was bent on pleasing Christ. He went from persecuting Christians to becoming one of them and, in time, one of the greatest apologists of the faith in the history of the church. The essence of the change in Paul was one of allegiance. Before, he gave his allegiance to the traditions of the Jews and the law as interpreted by them. When he met Christ, what he previously valued became like rubbish (Philippians 3:7-10). When doing mission work among the Gentiles, he was able to set aside the Jewish traditions in order that the preaching of the gospel might have preeminence (1 Colossians 9:19-23), demonstrating his allegiance to Christ.

With these two components of salvation in mind, position and allegiance, the questions in the second questionnaire can now be examined from a theological perspective.

Before and After Assessment Regarding Crop Failure

TABLE 10.1
Crop Failure

	Before		After	
	Yes	No	Yes	No
1. It's just fate.	135 (84.4%)	25 (15.6%)	98 (61.3%)	62 (38.7%)
2. The spirits of the dead were not appeased first.	55 (34.4%)	105 (65.5%)	18 (11.2%)	142 (88.8%)
3. The patron saint gets angry.	45 (28.1%)	115 (71.9%)	19 (11.9%)	141 (88.1%)
4. Evil spirits were not appeased first.	46 (28.9%)	113 (70.1%)	6 (3.7%)	155 (96.3%)

This table gives the reasons as to why the AG people believe that the crops sometimes fail. The left hand column represents what they believed before they became Christians and the right hand column indicates what they now believe. All research on causes of crop failure here revealed a significant difference in the AG people's views before and after they came to know Christ. In all cases, a positive paradigm shift had taken place in their lives. When they were given the opportunity to provide additional answers, thirty said that before they knew Christ they would have blamed the weather or the soil.

In comparing the responses, once they were saved the majority were less inclined to blame the weather, perform Catholic rituals such as praying the rosary or lighting candles, or to feel the need to appease spirits. They were, however, more inclined to admit that crop failure came as a lack of being faithful to God. To several respondents, this unfaithfulness means a lack of prayer or giving tithes. Whether they feared God's wrath is an open question, but their responses definitely indicate a belief in supernatural causality where God brings judgment because of lack of faithfulness to him.

In comparing the before and after responses here, the vast majority used to believe that crop failure was simply bad luck or one's fate in life. A rather significant minority felt that crops failed because of lack of sacrificing to various members of the spirit world. When they became Christians, however, this percentage dropped noticeably. A clear change has taken place in their thinking. Because of their salvation experience, they no longer feel the need to sacrifice to evil spirits and they recognized that idols are nothing to fear. Some understanding of their new position as believers has apparently come into their hearts, and they now know that they are children of God, no longer enslaved to the devil.

Several believers expressed that idea that crop failure can be a sign of God's displeasure, revealing a belief in supernatural causality. Not only is this belief rooted in Waray culture, it is also biblical. Passages such as Deuteronomy 28:58-68 clearly reveal that God does use crop failure and natural disaster to judge people for their sin.

Before and After Assessment Regarding the Spirits of the Dead

Before they received Christ, forty-five point one percent of the AG people believed that the dead can return to earth whereas after they became believers, only fourteen percent did so. The difference here is substantial, indicating that a major paradigm shift has taken place in their lives since they have come to know Jesus Christ. This is no doubt the biggest reason why sixty-nine percent of the AG population does not go to the gravesite on All Saints' Day, as opposed to only seven point six percent of the GP who do not go (see chapter six). AG people no longer fear the spirits because they no longer believe that the dead can return.

This table reflects a fundamental shift in the thinking of the AG respondents about whether the dead can return to earth. The fact that eighty-six percent no longer believe that the dead can return should not be understood as a denial of the spirit world. The change in their thinking may be the result of doing Bible studies on this issue, perhaps along the lines of what was written earlier in this chapter. Since the dead cannot return, at least on their own, there is no biblical reason to fear them. Because so many people have experienced or witnessed God's power to heal and deliver from demons, God's goodness has given them confidence in him. In this case, then, it can be said that learning and experiencing the truth can be applied to their felt need for protection from the dead. Since fear is a major factor here, it would seem that their new found faith in Jesus Christ has helped them to overcome this fear.

Before and After Assessment Regarding the Holy Spirit

TABLE 10.2
The Holy Spirit

	Before (477 Resp.)		After (478 Resp.)	
	Yes	No	Yes	No
1. I knew little or nothing about the Holy Spirit.	397 (83.2%)	80 (16.8%)	124 (25.9%)	354 (74.1%)
2. That the Holy Spirit is just like the other spirits in that he can heal people through the spiritist.	203 (42.9%)	270 (52.1%)	57 (11.9%)	421 (88.1%)
3. That the Holy Spirit is God.	359 (75.7%)	115 (24.3%)	463 (97.5%)	12 (2.5%)
4. That the Holy Spirit possesses all who trust in God and abides with them forever.	290 (60.8%)	187 (39.2%)	461 (96.6%)	16 (3.4%)
5. That every believer can be baptized in the Holy Spirit and speak in unknown tongues.	133 (27.9%)	344 (72.1%)	438 (91.6%)	40 (8.4%)

The differences in what they believed before they came to Christ and afterwards are significant on all five questions. The results are hardly surprising and, again, give evidence of a tremendous change in the thinking of the AG people since they became followers of Jesus Christ. Most of the respondents indicated that they knew little or nothing about the Holy Spirit before coming to Christ, although they did recognize him as a spirit being. Now almost three quarters of them say that is no longer true, indicating that they have learned about Him. This knowledge is reflected in the rest of their responses. In all questions, the responses of the AG people much more closely resemble what the Bible teaches regarding the Holy Spirit once they became believers. Why this may be so will be examined later.

The one response that is a bit surprising is that so many said that they knew that believers could be filled with the Holy Spirit and speak in tongues *before* they themselves became believers. This percentage is higher than in the first question where they indicated that they were familiar with the person and work of the Holy Spirit before they became believers. How can this be? Since *tambalans* use *orasyons*, prayers that are believed to be in Latin and, therefore, unintelligible to the hearer, perhaps some may confuse this with speaking in other tongues. A second explanation is that these respondents may have had friends and relatives who preceded them into a Pentecostal church who may have related their experience with the Holy Spirit to them.

Table 10.2 again gives strong evidence of a belief in the spirit world even before they became believers. In statement number two, forty-two point nine percent of the AG respondents said that before they came to Christ, they believed that the Holy Spirit was just like the other spirits used by the spiritists to bring healing. This is not a biblical position, as eighty-eight point one percent of them now recognize. In statements three and four, the majority believed in the deity of the Holy Spirit before they were saved and that he abides with believers forever. They most likely, however, did not understand this well since it is impossible for the mind of the unregenerate to understand the ways of the Spirit. Now almost all of them believe that the Holy Spirit is God who lives in those who trust in God and abide in him. This is the biblical position as reflected in John 14-16, suggesting that the pastors and workers who are discipling the AG Waray have done their work well. The contrasting traditional Waray belief, common to animists, is that the spirits come and go at their own pleasure.

Assemblies of God believers also give evidence of a greater understanding of the issue of speaking in tongues. This is solidly in line with biblical teaching that is based on Acts 2:1-4; 10:1-11:18, Acts 19:1-6 and many other portions of the Old and New Testaments.

Attempting to explain how this transformation in thinking has taken place is a bit difficult. Only a few pastors in Table 2.2 on page 33 indicated that they taught on the Holy Spirit in home Bible studies or recommended this subject for teaching in a church planting situation. Since the pastors interviewed were not given time to prepare for the interview, it may be that more pastors teach on this subject but didn't think about it when we spoke with them. Surely many pastors also preach and teach on this subject in the regular course of their pulpit ministry because good, biblical teaching is reflected in the data regarding this question.

Before and After Assessment Regarding Healing

TABLE 10.3
Healing

	Before (477 Resp.)		After (477 Resp.)	
	Yes	No	Yes	No
1. Went to a medical doctor?	405 (84.9%)	72 (15.1%)	349 (73.2%)	128 (26.8%)
2. Went to a witch-doctor?	269 (56.3%)	209 (43.7%)	30 (6.3%)	448 (93.7%)
3. Bought medicine?	458 (95.8%)	20 (4.2%)	421 (89.2%)	51 (10.8%)
	Yes	No	Yes	No
4. Went to a pastor or priest in the church for prayer?	81 (16.9%)	397 (83.1%)	399 (83.8%)	77 (16.2%)
5. Prayed directly to God and asked for healing?	401 (83.9%)	77 (16.1%)	478 (100%)	0 (0.0%)

The differences in how the AG people handled sickness before and after they came to Christ are statistically significant on all questions. Going to a medical doctor or buying medicine is not theologically important, but once people become believers there is a reduced tendency to go to the doctor or to buy medicine, perhaps suggesting that some would prefer just to trust God than go to a doctor. Also, now that they are believers, they are much more likely to go to their pastor for prayer than to the witchdoctor for treatment. This suggests that they maintain their belief in the power of the supernatural, albeit from a different source. The largest differences in this before and after comparison of treatments used for illness is the almost total abandoning of Mary, the saints and other spirits and the increased devotion to God. The other issues regarding taking care of oneself are about the same.

There has obviously been a tremendous paradigm shift in the lives of the AG people. It seems that the issue boils down to allegiance given to God after witnessing the power of God. In Table 10.4 below, which will be commented on in greater detail in the following paragraphs, nearly sixty-six percent said that they came to Christ as a result of being healed and forty point four percent said that deliverance from demons was part of their salvation experience. When the AG respondents saw or experienced the power of God, they were drawn to place their allegiance in Christ. In the context of Waray animism, demonstrations of the power of God got their attention. Through these miracles, God revealed himself to these people as one who could be trusted as worthy of their allegiance.

Key Elements in Coming to Christ

TABLE 10.4

Key Elements	Yes	No
Someone shared the gospel with you individually.	397 (83.4%)	79 (16.6%)
You received Christ when you heard a sermon or attended a Bible study.	431 (90.2%)	47 (9.8%)
You were healed.	311 (65.8%)	162 (34.2%)
You were delivered from a demon.	193 (40.4%)	295 (59.2%)
You experienced some other kind of miracle.	321 (67.3%)	156 (32.7%)
Someone demonstrated the love of God to you by helping you in practical ways.	394 (83.5%)	78 (16.5%)

Why the Waray Came to Christ

For this question all 477 respondents gave more than one answer to this question, suggesting, perhaps, that they see salvation as a process more than as a single event. A simple analysis is that hearing the Word of God, experiencing a miracle or having the love of God demonstrated in a practical way, were all key elements in bringing these respondents to Christ. Additionally, twenty-one added that they were saved through reading the Bible. In an animistic society such as the Philippines, all of these factors combine to make a potent witness for Christ.

In chapter three, many of the pastors testified how that miracles played a role in their ministry among the Waray. Healing was the kind of miracle most often mentioned and a several mentioned deliverance from demons and witchcraft, suggesting that there is a fair level of agreement between what the pastors said was helpful to them in their ministries and what believers say was important in bringing them to Christ. Regarding methodology, many said they received Christ through personal evangelism or attending a Bible study which correlates well with the pastor's assessment of these methods in Table 2.1 on page 27.

According to Table 10.4, the vast majority received Christ when someone verbally shared the gospel with them, whether it was during a home Bible study, at church, an evangelistic rally or in a one-on-one dialogue with a Christian. Most of them also experienced some sort of miracle such as healing or deliverance from demons. Their experience is a reminder of the ministry disciples whom Jesus sent out to preach the gospel, heal the sick, and raise the dead as evidence that the Kingdom of God had come to earth (Matthew 10:5-9). Through the preaching of the Word of God and through the power of the Spirit of God, the Kingdom of God has come to the Waray.

AG respondents also stated that they were drawn to Christ through a tangible expression of God's love to them. This is evidence that the AG believers were walking in obedience to John 13:34 and James 2:15-16.

When the body of Christ is walking in love according to what God intended, the church itself becomes God's compassionate good news, providing a powerful and tangible experience of love to nonbelievers. The world has no equal to the Church when it is functioning as it should.

I am convinced that the ministry of the Word, signs and wonders, and practical expressions of the love of God should be done in combination with each other. All of the evidence here points to an approach to bringing people into the Kingdom of God that involves four separate but related encounters. A power encounter is helpful in getting people's attention and encouraging their allegiance. But a power encounter alone is insufficient in communicating divine revelation. In the New Testament, both the Lord and the apostles performed miracles in conjunction with their teaching. While a power encounter reveals what God can do as well as who he is, a truth encounter through the anointed teaching of God's Word gives greater understanding of who he is and what he wants to do in the lives of believers. Allegiance is the third encounter. People must be confronted with the need to choose Christ and follow him or continue to walk in their animistic ways. The two paths are distinct and do not intertwine. The fourth encounter is a love encounter, showing God's love to people in a tangible way such as giving food or medicine. All of these elements contribute to providing an atmosphere where people are positively encouraged to give their allegiance to Christ, trusting in his power for healing and deliverance, trusting in his teaching to reveal his character and plan for their lives, and learning to trust in his love through the ministry of the Body of Christ.

In summary, the AG respondents reveal through their responses that they have had a genuine salvation experience where they have been transferred from the kingdom of darkness into the kingdom of light (Colossians 1:13). Because of this transfer, they now know the power of God to keep them safe from the devil and his troops as well as from the clutches of sin. They have also experienced a transformation in their allegiance, now entrusting their lives to Jesus Christ.

Chapter 11

CONCLUSIONS AND RECOMMENDATIONS

Having now identified the religious views of the Waray and having compared the views of the GP and AG populations with one another and with the Scriptures, some missiological implications related to contextualization, as well as conclusions and recommendations, can now be explained.

Missiological Implications Drawn From Kraft's Worldview Model

In Kraft's (1979:54-57) worldview model that was mentioned in chapter five on pages 84-86, he articulates five functions of worldview: explanation, evaluation, psychological reinforcement, integration and adaptation. Keeping in mind that the definition of contextualization in use here is that of presenting the gospel to the Waray within their own cultural context and worldview, without compromising the message, application can now be made toward the goal of contextualization by using Kraft's functions.

Explanation

Kraft (1979:54) writes:

> The first function is the *explanation* of how and why things got to be as they are and how and why they continue or change. The worldview embodies for a people, whether explicitly or implicitly, the basic assumptions concerning ultimate things on which they base their lives.

The worldview of the GP is heavily animistic, their basic assumptions about life being focused on the supernatural. The universe is conceived to be a place controlled by capricious supernatural beings. For example, when someone gets sick, the sickness may have been caused by a spirit. Crop failure may be explained as the work of disgruntled ancestors. The *tambalan* plays an important role in Waray society as one who stands between the realm of the spirits and the role of men, determining the will of the spirits and attempting to manipulate them to do the will of man. People will also pray to the saints or the Virgin to get what they want. One must agree with Maggay's (1998:365) conclusion that "Filipino religion remains primarily a transaction of the powers."

The worldview of the AG population is also heavily supernatural as evidenced by their responses to the questionnaires. But it also reflects a world where an omnipotent God is in control. For the AG, reality can be explained with God at the focus. He controls the weather and the crops. He also heals. When protection is needed from demons, the AG believers find that the name of the Lord is a strong tower (Proverbs 18:10) and, from that vantage point can explain that demons are subservient to the name of Jesus Christ (Philippians 2:9-11). Maggay's point about the "transaction of power" is also validated among the AG population, but God is at the center of the transaction.

Evaluation

Kraft (1979:55) notes that for most cultures of the world, the ultimate ground of determining values, institutions, and customs is the supernatural, their worldview being validated by their view of God. The Waray are no exception, their values, customs and tradition validating and being validated by their worldview.

To bring change to their worldview, change must first be made to their view of God. When their view of God is changed, they will then be willing and able to evaluate their values and customs. This has already happened to the overwhelming majority of the AG population. On most issues, the differences between the AG and the GP were substantial. Even though there was substantial agreement between the two groups on the issue of demon possession, there were large differences between them on the related issue of protecting oneself from demons (Table 9.1 on page 149). Again, the differences stem from the transformation that has taken place in the thinking of the AG population.

In looking at the responses of the members and adherents on the various questions there is evidence that this evaluation process is still in progress in the lives of the adherents, and that their values and activities may in fact be closer to the GP than the members. There is every reason to think that the process of transformation in their thinking will be completed as long as they continue to study the Scriptures and grow in their faith. As they move along this continuum, they will continue the process of reevaluating their past values and customs in light of God's word. Some may revert to the old ways while others will press on to maturity in Christ. One must also assume that as more Waray embrace the gospel their path to transformation will be similar to that of the members and adherents studied here. The gospel, which must be communicated within a culture in order to be understood, also becomes an agent of cultural transformation.

Psychological Reinforcement

Kraft (1979:55) states that:

At points of anxiety or crisis in life it is to one's conceptual system that one turns for the encouragement to continue or the stimulus to take other action. Crisis times such as death, birth, and illness; transition times such as puberty, marriage, planting and harvest; times of uncertainty. . . . all tend to heighten anxiety or in some other way require adjustment between behavior and belief.

Evidence of this truth is abundant throughout this study. In times of trouble the GP pray to the saints or the Virgin Mary and, when sick, go to the witchdoctor as well as the medical doctor.

By contrast, the AG population, by and large, prays to God alone in times of trouble, such as drought, and does not go to the witchdoctor when sick. When feeling the need for protection, AG people are much more likely to go to their pastor or go directly to God in prayer than they are to use an amulet. What this indicates is that there is a new reference point in their worldview to which they turn for comfort and help in times of crisis. As they continue to grow and mature in Christ and respond in a biblical manner in times of trouble or crisis, their confidence in God will continue to grow, thus reinforcing their new worldview.

Integration

Kraft (1979:56) explains the idea of integration:

> The worldview of a culture or subculture serves an *integrating* function. It systematizes and orders for them their perceptions of reality into an overall design. In terms of this integrated and integrating perspective, then, a people conceptualizes what reality should be like and understands and interprets the multifarious events to which they are exposed.

The Waray's animistic worldview orders their perceptions of reality. When something out of the ordinary happens, it makes perfect sense to them to relate it to the supernatural. Because they perceive the universe as being controlled by powerful supernatural beings that can bless or curse, they pray to them, making whatever vows are deemed necessary to secure their blessings. They also appease them through sacrifices to avoid their wrath. In these instances and many others like them, order is brought to the world of the Waray, giving them a perception of reality that is integrated within their worldview.

When the Waray receive Christ, a paradigm shift begins to take place in their thinking. They no longer accept the legitimacy of the claims made about the power of the Virgin Mary, the saints or any of the spirits. They still accept, however, the reality of supernatural powers that may not control the universe, but are still active in the affairs of men. While the GP believes that these supernatural powers can be benevolent or malevolent, it seems that the AG population now believes that these powers, except for God himself, are malevolent.

What, then, is the evidence of new integrating factors that hold together this paradigm shift in the worldview of the AG population? This question can first be answered by what they no longer do. Because they no longer feel the need to appease the spirits, they no longer offer sacrifices. They no longer the feel the need to pray to the Virgin or the saints. They no longer feel a great need to wear amulets, trusting God alone instead for their protection. If they go to the gravesite or attend the fiesta, they are more likely to go for social rather than religious reasons. In other words, the old way of integrating saints, spirits and sacrifices does not fit the new paradigm, which is focused on God and his son, Jesus Christ.

The primary integrating factor, in this case, is God himself. The AG people have come into a new, dynamic relationship with him, causing a paradigm shift in their beliefs and values. But this paradigm shift in worldview often causes conflict or dissonance with the old ways. The old values, institutions, customs, and actions must then be re-evaluated to see if they can be integrated into the new paradigm or whether they must be rejected.

The research reveals that as the Waray experience the reality of God's gracious saving power, both in personal reconciliation with him and in healing, deliverance, protection and provision, they naturally exchange their old worldview for something better. As one AG respondent told one of our researchers about her conversion to Christ, "I found out that God is good."

The research also reveals that as the Waray continue in their study of the Scripture and in their relationship to God through Christ, the old life paradigm becomes increasingly irrelevant. This is probably why AG pastors found no need to immediately teach on the issue of idolatry at the beginning of the discipleship process. Rather than risk a breakdown in relationships, pastors wait until the Waray have already understood and experienced something of God's goodness, power and uniqueness. Then they are open to teaching that contradicts the old paradigm because they have already begun to embrace a biblical worldview. However, the biblical teaching on idolatry should not be avoided. More will be said about this a little later.

Here, one must part company with Catholic scholars such as Mercado (1992), Beltran (1987), Bulatao (1992:69) and the CBCP (1997), whose entire works are built on the belief that cultural values should be accommodated even if they are not in line with the Scriptures. For example the conviction shared by Bulatao (1992:70) and Belita (1991:97), as well as the CBCP (1997:249-250), that idolatry is permissible because it accords well with Filipino culture must be rejected on biblical grounds.

The Catholic scholars, however, have argued that since Filipinos, including the Waray, value a God who is immanent, whom they can see and touch, they need images.

One of the significant findings of the research is just over eighty-three percent of the AG people came to Christ because Christians showed love to them. This fact, together with the Waray's' felt need for an immanent God, has profound implications for evangelism and discipleship. A tremendously beneficial study for the both the Waray and other lowland Filipinos could be done on the doctrine of Christians becoming conformed to the image of Christ, especially as it is found in Romans 8:30. Since Jesus proclaimed that Christians' love for one another would be the mark that sets them apart as his disciples before the world in John 13:36, training and encouragement to care for others would meet this felt need for love. But the fact that when Christians love one another, God lives in us and his love is made complete (I John 4:12) also meets the needs to experience the immanence of God—in the faces, hands and words of Christ's followers who bear his image.

The old customs which are biblical or at least do not violate the Scriptures can and should be retained as there is no reason why believers cannot also be Waray. Those values that do not measure up the Scriptures must be amended or rejected. In some cases, customs that must be rejected can be replaced with a functional substitute that will bring honor to God and also fit within the Waray culture. A case in point is that every church has an annual church anniversary thanksgiving service that could be used as an alternative to the fiesta. The essential components of the fiesta are food, games, dancing and thanksgiving to the patron saint. Thus it is both a spiritual and a social event. On a church's anniversary, there is plenty of food and lots of games and worshipful dancing in some areas of the country. But instead of honoring the patron saint, worship and honor is given to God. Integration into the new paradigm has taken place here in that what is biblical (the idea of thanksgiving and celebration) has been retained, what is not unbiblical (i.e. eating and playing games) is allowed. Giving thanks to the patron saint, which is not biblical, has been changed to that which is, giving thanks to God.

Adaptation

Concerning adaptation Kraft (1979:56) writes:

> People do on occasion shift in their perceptions of reality. They come to see things in ways slightly or drastically different from the ways that their worldview has conditioned them to perceive of them. They change one or more of their conceptual models and reinterpret their perceptions. And such shifts in perception, especially if engaged in and reported by socially influential persons, may be accepted by other members of their

social group. This results in groups altering their conceptual structuring, their models of reality.

The truth of this regarding the AG population among the Waray has been well documented. People do change. As people within a culture change, the culture itself changes. But in order for change to come about, people must understand how the change will benefit them. Changes, then, must be understood within the current cultural framework. In other words, in order to encourage people to change their views of reality, the gospel must be presented to people within their current perceptions of the way things are. As believers share their faith in a culturally relevant manner that demonstrates how Jesus Christ alone can meet their felt needs, those that are most open to change will likely be the most receptive to the message.

Kraft (1979:56) notes that this transformation normally takes place slowly. Jesus himself said that "the kingdom of heaven is like yeast that a woman took and mixed into a large amount of flour until it worked all through the dough" (Matthew 13:33). As the yeast gradually changes the texture of bread, so the gospel can change the worldview and destiny of the Waray people.

Hypothesis Proven

The hypothesis undertaken in this study, that the religious beliefs of the Waray are steeped in animism and folk Catholicism, that the Assemblies of God grew and developed by preaching the gospel, accompanied by demonstrations of the power of God in healing and deliverance from demonic powers and that contact points can be drawn between the Waray belief system and biblical teaching that will enable the gospel to be presented to the Waray. This has been proven throughout the research.

Answering the Research Questions

With the knowledge of the Waray religious beliefs and what the Bible says about them firmly in mind, the research questions posed in the Introduction can now be answered.

What are the Religious Beliefs of the Waray as They Pertain to Their Animistic Practices?

The religious beliefs of the Waray reflect a strong belief in the presence and power of the supernatural and that supernatural beings are active in the world today. These beliefs are particularly manifest in the Waray's views of the origins of sickness, the power to heal, the need to wear amulets, the fear of demonic possession and, to a much lesser extent because of the fewer number of people involved, the need to conduct rituals in planting and harvesting crops.

In many cases, Roman Catholicism and animistic practices were mixed together. Examples from this research could be found in leaving an offering for the dead at the gravesite to ensure the blessing of the dead upon the living or at least to avoid being cursed by them. In most of these cases, the attitudes of the AG population were substantially different from the GP, the AG reflecting attitudes more in the line with the Scriptures.

What Were the Elements of the Gospel That Contributed to the Growth and Development of the Assemblies of God Churches Among the Waray?

The answer to this question is found primarily in Table 10.4 on page 174, but is also hinted at on Table 2.2 on page 33. Here, nearly sixty-six percent of the respondents said that healing was part of their salvation experience. Forty percent also said that deliverance from demons helped bring them to Christ. This suggests that the power of God played a strong role in the salvation experience of many respondents. The research here accords well with Maggay (1999:24), who notes that the growth of the Charismatic movement, with it's emphasis on the power manifestations of the Spirit, is not an accident, connecting well to a culture whose religion is power oriented. Many Waray who came to Christ experienced a power encounter.

The same table also reveals that the vast majority of the AG population received Christ through someone's testimony or through an exposition of the Scriptures in Bible study or in church. Similarly, several indicated that they were saved through personal Bible reading, media programs, or evangelistic crusades. This agrees well with the pastors' statements that house-to-house evangelism, evangelistic crusades with follow-up and home Bible studies (see Table 2.1 on page 27 were among their most effective forms of evangelism.

Through these methods, people were confronted with the truth of God's word regarding salvation. The doctrine of salvation itself was the pastor's favorite subject in the Bible studies. While the pastors did not give the details regarding what they taught about salvation, the evidence suggests that, in one way or another, they taught that salvation is a change of allegiance. Since salvation is based on what Christ has done, thereby giving him the preeminence to which he is entitled, the pastors seem to agree with Dominguez and Dominguez (1989:27) that contextualization should be centered on Jesus Christ. God alone, and not the Virgin Mary or the saints, is worthy of our trust, adoration and obedience. So the Waray also experienced a truth encounter.

The research undertaken here suggests that not only must Christ be the focus of our teaching, what is taught about him must be clearly articulated. Beltran's (1987:206) caution about being overly articulate in this regard because Filipinos, in this case the Waray, are intuitive, is misleading. It is true that intuition is important in religious experience. An intimate experience with God, which is sometimes difficult to describe in human language, is desirable for a vibrant faith. Nevertheless, divine revelation must be expressed clearly in order for people to come to a true faith in the true Christ.

Having said this, God's word must be communicated in a format conducive to the Waray's way of thinking. Teaching through stories and anecdotes and the use of visual aids, even among adults, is much easier for the Waray than through the linear logic based sermons that tend to dominate Western pulpits.

In Table 10.4 on page 174, eighty-three point five percent of the AG sample population received Christ because someone expressed the love of God to them in practical ways. The pastors agreed, at least to an extent. In Table 2.1 on page 27, some of the pastors listed practical ways in which they ministered to people. While not many in number, they do represent ways of sharing the love of Christ with people in a viable expression of John 3:16. Sharing God's love with the Waray in a practical way not only meets physical needs, but is in accord with the Waray's propensity to be highly sociable, and open to a love encounter with Christ and his followers. When the Waray experienced God's power, learned his truth and saw his love in action, they were led into a fourth encounter, allegiance and placed their trust in Christ alone.

What Comparisons Might be Made Between Biblical Theology and the Religious Belief System of the Waray?

The strongest favorable comparison is in the area of supernatural power. This is evidenced by their responses in chapter nine. Because of their animistic worldview, the Waray are open to the power of the supernatural, especially when it comes to miracles such as healing. But their worldview also leads to a great fear of evil spirits. The power of God to heal and deliver from demons is a core belief of the Assemblies of God. God heals because he is all-powerful and because healing is part of the atonement. He delivers people from demonic power in demonstration of his lordship of the spirit world. The Bible's message of healing and deliverance is good news to the Waray. In summary, the research questions have been satisfactorily answered.

Recommendations for Further Study

Because healing is a large issue to the Waray, further research could be done in the area of the healing deities in biblical times and what the Bible has to say about them. This could then be compared to the folk healing practices done among the Waray with the intent of bringing deeper teaching in this area to the believers with greater maturity as a result.

The process of transformation or paradigm shift that takes place in the hearts and of the Waray as they embrace Christ, which has been mentioned many times throughout the course of this study, needs to be researched in greater detail with the goal of improving the discipleship process in order to make this transformation complete in the lives of the people.

Further research regarding how exactly the pastors deal with the issue of images, amulets, and talismans, especially what kind of deliverance ministry is involved, would be beneficial to developing Bible study tools and deliverance ministry guidelines that will help in the transformation process of new believers, as well as illustrate the power of the gospel to unbelievers.

This study has focused on contextualization as it relates to the proclamation of the gospel. Also, some of the felt needs of the Waray may not have been adequately addressed. A more complete effort at contextualization is needed, preferably to be done by the Waray themselves, which would evaluate all of the customs, values and felt needs of the Waray in light of the Scriptures.

Recommendations For Practical Ministry

Many of the Waray came to Christ through a power encounter. The implication of this is that those sharing the gospel with the Waray need to take seriously the command of Jesus to heal and teach (Matthew 10:7-8). This requires that the help of the Holy Spirit be sought for a ministry that strikes at the heart of the Waray's need for power in their lives. The Apostle Paul said that the Kingdom of God is not "a matter of talk but of power" (I Corinthians 4:20). Prayer is needed to seek God for miracles which confirm the Word of God (Mark 16:18-20) in conformity with the pattern of ministry that Jesus taught us.

One area that could not be measured completely in this study is the depth of the AG population's understanding of the person and work of the Holy Spirit. They need to be taught that he is not like the other spirits that take possession of people to their own destruction and then leave when they have no further use for that person. The Holy Spirit abides with the believer forever, and it is to the believer's advantage that he does so (John 14-16). Even though the interviews suggest that the people have a good grasp on the basics of the doctrine of the Spirit, the evidence suggests they need a deeper understanding.

While the AG respondents were asked if they believed in the baptism in the Holy Spirit (Table 10.2 on page 170), they were not asked if they had personally experienced it. Further research here would be desirable to determine how great the need might be for people to experience this baptism. Because of the Waray's orientation to the spirit world, pastors are encouraged to preach often about the baptism in the Holy Spirit and pray for each and every believer to be filled. They should then be encouraged to "keep on being filled with the Spirit," to sing to themselves with songs and hymns and spiritual songs (Ephesians 5:18-19), to pray in tongues (1 Corinthians 14), to pray in the Spirit (Ephesians 6:18) and to turn away from every dark, frightening or depressing idea to the truth of the Word of God. They also must be encouraged to get rid of any object has any animistic connotations because they must make a complete break from the old life and the spirits in order to press on to maturity in Christ. To this end, Bible Studies or Sunday School classes where they study the Old Testament books such as Genesis, Exodus, and Leviticus and many of the Scriptures mentioned will help them see clearly the freedom in the

Spirit they now have as opposed to the bondage they had under the gods of Egypt. They also need to see clearly that the sin of idolatry, witchcraft, fortune telling and all forms of association with evil spirits is an abomination to God.

A number of pastors said that they do not deal with idolatry even though it is a core issue of their worldview. To negate it is to ignore the issue of allegiance, which is central to the gospel of Jesus Christ.

Once people are filled with the Spirit, they need to be taught to walk in the Spirit, which includes living out the fruit (Galatians. 5:22-23; 1 Corinthians. 13). In conjunction with spiritual gifts, it would be wise to teach the fruit of the Spirit with clear understanding that it is not a person's "good character" or strong decision to be good that produce this fruit, but rather a willingness to surrender to the Holy Spirit who is at work in the Christian. An emphasis on loving could serve to deepen the love encounter of new believers as well as show what a fruitful life in the Spirit looks like. As mentioned earlier, since the chief commandment Jesus left his disciples is that we love one another, and since we experience God's love and presence through this love (John 13:34-35), a series of studies could be developed about what it means for believers to be conformed to Christ's image in their relationships with one another. This could greatly contribute to the Waray's need for immanence in their relationship with God as well as bring healing and growth to individuals, families and church relationships.

Table 2.2 on page 33 also revealed a paucity of teaching on the spiritual disciplines such as prayer, fasting, tithing, and the need to daily read the Bible. While some of these would not be appropriate in a Bible study with unbelievers, they are essential to laying a good foundation in the lives of new believers. This table also revealed no teaching on issues related to the family. New believers in particular need to be taught godly principles of marriage and parenting, as well as being reminded the Bible affirms the Waray value of respecting their elders in areas that do not lead to compromise with their new faith. The list of subjects taught in home Bible studies reveals a good emphasis on many other subjects. What I did not find, however, was any kind of systematic Bible study whereby the people are taught the various doctrines of Scriptures in an organized manner, nor did I discover any emphasis on teaching hermeneutics.

Recommendations For the Broader Application of the Results of This Study

Because of the similarities in worldview among the lowland Filipino cultures, this study has a broad application throughout the Philippine lowlands. Pastors could use the results of this study to teach their people what the Bible says about the doctrinal issues elucidated here, although this study might be more usable to them in a storytelling format in simple English or, preferably, in the vernacular. Among the more purely animistic people groups of the Philippines, which are a relatively small minority and among Filipino Muslims, many of the theological issues studied here are relevant. These include healing, deliverance from demons, God's attitude towards divination, and what the Bible has to say about the dead returning, the biblical concept of blessing and cursing, as well as God's control over creation.

Fourth, I see a great need for Evangelicals and Pentecostals to enter the academic debates on contextualization going on in the Philippines, as this area is almost completely dominated by Catholic scholars. This book is intended to be a contribution to this effort.

Conclusion

The problem that has been addressed in this research was to identify elements in the worldview of the Waray people of the Leyte/Samar region of the Philippines that could be useful for the development of a contextual theology through a historical study of the founding and growth of the Assemblies of God, and an analysis of the Waray worldview and religious beliefs.

The issue was addressed through background research on the Waray culture and worldview in chapter three, which established the major worldview issues for examination. Questions were drawn from the precedent research and put into questionnaires, each question to a correlating theological theme.

Chapter one told the story of the history and development of the Assemblies of God among the Waray. In vivid detail, Pedro Sumulat, the first church planter among the Waray, told of his trials and triumphs, his failures and his successes. Others, too, related how God used them in ministry, particularly church planting, among the Waray. Zion Bible Institute was born out of a desire to evangelize the Waray and to train church planters. Even though the burden of church planting has now shifted to the Eastern Visayas District Council, the Bible school still has a critical role to play in discipling the next generation of pastors and leaders of Waray churches.

In chapter two, the AG pastors also related what subjects they taught and the methodologies they used to reach the Waray for Christ. They tended to teach on the basic doctrines of the Bible, as would be natural in any evangelistic or new believer's Bible study. The successful evangelism methodologies that they have employed such as home Bible studies, visitation, or a combination of these in connection with an evangelistic crusade, are reflective of the social values of face to face contact among the Waray. Radio ministry is the exception to this rule and yet has been successful in church planting.

In chapters five through ten, the results of the field research were tabulated and interpreted. The results revealed that both sample populations had a high view of the supernatural, both believed in the power of God and both groups reflected the conviction that demons can possess people. But the dissimilarities, however, outweighed the similarities. While the GP pray to God, they also pray to many others, including the Virgin Mary. While they believe that God can heal, they also believe that there are other supernatural beings that have the power as well.

By contrast, an average of ninety percent of the AG population disavow these other entities, claiming that God alone can hear and answer prayer, including healing the sick. The statistical differences between the GP and AG were astronomical in most cases. The small minority, among the AG, that still has values closer to the GP tended to be adherents.

In terms of the customs of going to the gravesite on All Saints' Day and attending the fiesta, the vast majority of the GP attend and participate in most of the related activities. The raw scores of the AG reflect a less than uniform opinion on these issues, although they still revealed substantially different values from those of the GP. What was clear, however, is that most, although not all, of the AG respondents who attend these events participate in the social rather than the religious aspects.

The data analyzed revealed substantial differences between the two populations on most of the issues covered. The GP revealed a mindset steeped in animism. The AG population, by contrast, revealed a significantly different way of thinking. Their mindset sees God at the center of the universe, suggesting that a paradigm shift has taken place. This shift is particularly obvious in the raw scores of Tables 10.1 to 10.3 on pages 168, 170 and 173 which contrasts their beliefs and practices before and after becoming believers.

The biblical gospel message must continue to be preached and taught among the Waray with signs and wonders following and with a body of believers who reflect Christ's loving character to others. Through these encounters, truth, power and love, the Waray will be able to hear the message well and give their allegiance to Christ.

REFERENCES CITED

Abayan, Primo
    2001   Interview with the author. Lawaan, Eastern Samar, December 4.

Alreck, Pamela L. and Settle, Robert B.
    1995   The Survey Research Handbook. 2nd Edition. New York: Irwin/McGraw Hill.

Alston, Mark
    2003   Email to the author December 12.
    2001   Interview with the author. Mandaluyong City, Metro Manila, October 31.

Arellano, Eduardo
    2001   "Why Favor a Dogma of Mary as Coredemptrix, Mediatrix, and Advocate?" in Theo Week II: Emerging Theological Themes. Pp. 194-232. Ed. Fausto B. Gomez and Benedict V. Reyes. Manila: University of Santo Tomas.

Arens, Richard
    1957   "The Use of Amulets and Talismans in Leyte and Samar." Journal of East Asiatic Studies. 6(April): 115-126.
    1982   Folk Practices and Beliefs of Leyte and Samar. Revised ed. Gregorio C. Luangco, ed. Tacloban City, Philippines: Divine Word University Press.

Arnold, Clinton
    1997   3 Questions About Spiritual Warfare. Grand Rapids: Baker Book House.
    1996   The Colossian Syncretism: The Interface Between Christianity and Folk Belief at Colossae. Grand Rapids: Baker Book House.
    1992   Power and Magic: the Concept of Power in Ephesians. Grand Rapids: Baker Book House.

Anacion, Dulce Cuna
    1991   "Yunal: The Orasyon Tattoo as Folk Practice and Art in Leyte." M.A. thesis, University of the Philippines.

Aune, David E.
    1979a   "Divination." In The International Standard Bible Encyclopedia. Vol. 1. Geoffrey Bromiley, ed. Pp. 971-974. Grand Rapids: William B. Eerdmans Publishing Company.

    1979b   "Demonology." In <u>The New International Standard Bible Encyclopedia</u>. Vol. 1. Geoffrey W. Bromiley, ed. Pp. 919-923. Grand Rapids: William B. Eerdmans Publishing Company

Babbie, Earl
    1990   <u>Survey Research Methods</u>. 2nd Edition. Belmont, CA: Wadsworth Publishing Company.

Barney, G. Linwood
    n.d.   "The Supracultural and the Cultural: Implications for Frontier Missions." Unpublished manuscript. Quoted in <u>Communicating Christ Cross-Culturally: An Introduction to Missionary Communication</u>. 2nd edition. David J. Hesselgrave, ed. Grand Rapids: Zondervan Publishing House, 1991.

Baclayan, Ben
    2001   Personal Interview with a researcher of the author. Biliran Island, December 5.

Balista, Gonie
    2001   Personal interview with the author. Libertad, Leyte, December 5.

Belita, Jaime
    1991   <u>The Way of Greater Self: Constructing a Theology Around a Filipino Mythos.</u> Manila: De La Salle University Press.

Beltran, Benigno
    1987   <u>The Christology of the Inarticulate: An Inquiry into the Filipino Understanding of Jesus Christ</u>. Manila: Divine Word Publications.

Berg, Bruce L.
    2001   <u>Qualitative Research Methods for the Social Sciences</u>. Boston: Allyn and Bacon. 4th Edition.

Besere, Naomi
    2001   Personal interview with the author. Alang-Alang, Leyte, November-December.

Black, Thomas R.
    1999   <u>Doing Quantitative Research in the Social Sciences: An Integrated Approach to Research Design, Measurement and Statistics</u>. Thousand Oaks, CA: Sage Publications.

Biron-Polo, Jaime
    1988   Rethinking Philippine Symbols: Moments of Domination and Resistence in the Province of Leyte. Quezon City: by the author.

Brown, Colin
    1986   "Miracle." In The International Standard Bible Encyclopedia. Vol. 3. Geoffrey W. Bromiley, ed. Pp. 371-381. Grand Rapids: William B. Eerdmans Publishing Company.

Brown, Michael L.
    1995   Israel's Divine Healer. Grand Rapids: Zondervan Publishing Company.

Bruce, F. F.
    1964   The Epistle to the Hebrews. The New International Commentary on the New Testament. F.F. Bruce, ed. Grand Rapids: William B. Eerdmans Publishing Company.

Cabangangan, Edong
    2001   Personal interview with the author. Calbayog, Western Samar, December 14.

Cagas, Roque
    2003   Personal interview with the author. Metro Manila, January 7.

Castino, Rening
    2001   Personal inteview with the author. Catbologan, Western Samar, November-December.

Catholic Bishop's Conference of the Philippines
    1997   Catechism for Filipino Catholics. Manila: ECCCE Word & Life Publications.

Contado, Mina E.
    1977   "Power Dynamics of Rural Families: The Case of A Samar Barrio." M.A. thesis, University of the Philippines at Los Banos.

Cruiz, Miriam
    2002   Personal interview with the author. Palo, Leyte, April 9.

Curtis, Jim
    2002   Personal interview with the author. Quezon City, Metro Manila, February 18.

Cuyco, Nicolasita
    1983   "A Study of Medicinal Plants in Lavizaris, N. Samar Used by Herbolarios to Treat Ailments: It's Implications to School Health Curriculum." M.A. thesis, University of Eastern Philippines.

De Mesa Jose M.
    1987   <u>In Solidarity With the Culture: Studies in Theological Re-rooting</u>. Quezon City: Maryhill School of Theology.

Demetrio, Francisco
    1975   "Philippine Shamanism and Southeast Asian Parallels." In <u>Dialogue for Development</u>. Fransciso Demetrio, ed. Pp. 679-716. Cagayan De Oro City: Xavier University.

Dominguez, Arsenio and Edith
    1989   <u>Theological Themes for the Filipino Church</u>. Quezon City: New Day Publishers.

Downie, N.M. and Heath, Robert W.
    1983   <u>Basic Statistical Methods</u>. 5th edition. New York: Harper and Row.

Edwards, David M.
    1979   "Affliction." In <u>The International Standard Bible Encyclopedia</u>. Vol. 1. Geoffrey W. Bromiley, ed. Pp. 61-62. Grand Rapids: William B. Eerdmans Publishing Company.

Eguia, Joey
    1989   "Marvels of His Grace in Region VIII." Unpublished manuscript.

Flemming, Dean
    2005   <u>Contextualization in the New Testament: Patterns for Theology and Mission</u>. Downer's Grove, IL: Inter-Varsity Press.

Gabato, Eva
    2001   Personal interview with the author's wife. Western Samar, November-December.

Gacoscosim, Maricel
    2001   Personal interview with the author's wife. Catbologan, Western Samar, November-December

Galvez-Tan, Jaime
    1977   "Religious Elements in Samar-Leyte Folk Medicine." In <u>Filipino Religious Psychology</u>. Leonardo N. Mercado, ed. Pp. 3-21. Tacloban City: Divine Word University Publications.

General Council of the Assemblies of God
    2003   <u>Minutes of the 50th Session of The General Council of the Assemblies of God With Revised Constitution and Bylaws</u>. Springfield, MO.

Gilliland, Dean., ed.
    1988   <u>The Word Among Us: Contextualizing Theology for Mission</u>

<u>Today</u>. Dallas: Word Publishing.

Harrison, Roland K.

    1982   "Heal." In <u>The New International Standard Bible Encyclopedia</u>. Vol. 3. Geoffrey W. Bromiley, ed. Pp. 640-646. Grand Rapids: William B. Eerdmans Publishing Company.

    1976   "Demon, Demoniac, Demonology." In <u>The Zondervan Pictorial Encyclopedia of the Bible</u>. Vol. 2. Merrill G. Tenney, ed. Pp. 93-101. Grand Rapids: Zondervan Publishing Company.

Henry, Rodney

    1986   <u>Filipino Spirit World: A Challenge to the Church</u>. Manila: OMF Publishers.

Hesselgrave, David J.

    1991   <u>Communicating Christ Cross-Culturally: An Introduction to Missionary Communication</u>. 2nd ed. Grand Rapids: Zondervan Publishing House.

Hocsen, Gloria G.

    1968   "A Survey of Prevailing Traditional Beliefs and Practices of the People of Merida, Leyte, and Their Educational Implications." M.A. thesis, Divine Word University, Tacloban City.

Huey, F. B., Jr.

    1976   "Idolatry." In <u>The Zondervan Pictorial Encyclopedia of the Bible</u>. Vol 3. Merrill C. Tenney, ed. Pp. 242-248. Grand Rapids: Zondervan Publishing Company.

Ibañez, Nena

    2001   Personal interview with the author. Santa Fe, Leyte, December 9.

Illuminado, Mernilo Jr.

    2001   Personal interview with the author. San Jose, Leyte, December 5.

Jadloc, Zosimo

    1988   "History and Kinship in a Waray Community." Ph.D dissertation, University of the Philippines

Jocano, F. Landa

    1981   <u>Folk Christianity: A Preliminary Study of Conversion and Patterning of Christian Experience in the Philippines</u>. Quezon City: Trinity College of Quezon City.

Johnson, David M.

2009 Led By The Spirit: The History of the American Assemblies of God Missionaries in the Philippines. Manila: ICI Ministries.

2000 "A Study of the Animistic Practices of the Waray People of the Leyte-Samar Region of the Philippines." M.A. thesis, Asia Pacific Theological Seminary.

Keener, Craig S.
- 1993 The IVP Bible Background Commentary: New Testament. Downer's Grove, IL: Inter-Varsity Press.

Kraft, Charles H.
- 1979 Christianity in Culture: A Study in Dynamic Biblical Tehologizing in Cross-Cultural Perspective. Marynoll, NY: Orbis Books.

Kobak, Cantius. J.
- 1978 "Death Rituals and Burial Practices in Leyte and Samar." Leyte-Samar Studies 12(2):41-60.

Lane, William L.
- 1991 Hebrews 1-8. Word Biblical Commentary, Vol 47a. David A. Hubbard and Glenn W. Barker, eds. Dallas, TX: Word Books.

Lapura, Cruz
- 2001 Personal interview with the author. Catbologan, Western Samar, November-December.

Lasaga, Mimi
- 2002 Personal interview with the author. Palo, Leyte, April 9.

Lee, Richard
- 2000 The Healing Touch of Jesus: God's Power and Passion to Make You Whole. West Monroe, LA: Howard Publishing Company.

Leitch, Addison. H.
- 1976 "Mediator, Mediation." In The Zondervan Pictorial Encyclopedia of the Bible. Vol 3. Merrill C. Tenney, ed. Pp. 150-158. Grand Rapids: Zondervan Publishing House.

Licauco, Jaime
- 1982 The Magicians of God: The Amazing Stories of Philippine Folk Healers. Manila: National Bookstore.

Liefeld, Walter E.
- 1976 "Divination." In the Zondvervan Pictorial Encyclopedia of the Bible. Vol 2. Merrill C. Tenney, ed. Pp. 146-149. Grand Rapids: Zondervan Publishing Company.

Liguarda, Andres
    1997   Personal Interview with the author. Canavid, Eastern Samar, May 15.

Lua, Theresa R.
    1998   "Developing a Holistic and Contextualized Discipleship Ministry Among Filipino Urban Poor Adults in Metro Manila." Ed.D. dissertation, Asia Graduate School of Theology.

Maggay, Melba P.
    2011   <u>A Clash of Cultures: Early American Protestant Missions and Filipino Religious Consciousness</u>. Manila: Anvil Publishing, Inc.
    1999   "Towards Sensitive Engagement with Filipino Indigenous Conciousness." <u>International Review of Missions</u> 87 (346): 361-371.
    1989   <u>Communicating Cross-Culturally: Towards a New Context for Missions in the Philippines</u>. Quezon City: New Day Publishing.

Martinez, Christina J.
    1990   "The Linambay of Linao: a Study of Theater as Ritual." M.A. thesis: University of the Philippines.

Matiga, Lemuel
    2001   Personal Interview with the author. Dulag, Leyte, December 7, 2001.

Matiga, Vaden
    2002   Personal Interview with the author. Palo, Leyte, April.

Mercado, Leonardo M.
    1992   <u>Inculturation and Filipino Theology</u>. Manila: Divine Word Publications.
    1976   <u>Elements of Filipino Philosophy</u>. Tacloban City: Divine Word University Publications.
    1975   <u>Elements of Filipino Theology</u>. Tacloban City: Divine Word University Publications.

Merriam-Webster
    1993   <u>Merriam Webster's Collegiate Dictionary</u>. Tenth Edition.

Mertons, Donna M.
    1997   <u>Research Methods in Education and Psychology: Integrating Diversity with Quantitiative & Qualitative Approaches</u>. Thousand Oaks, CA: Sage Publications.

Miranda-Feliciano, Evelyn
   1990   <u>Filipino Values and Our Christian Faith</u>. Manila: OMF Publishers, Inc.

Molina, Totie
   2001   Personal interview with the author. Capoocan, Leyte, December 8.

Montes, Levi
   2002   Personal interview with the author. Palo, Leyte, April 8.

Mundle, Wilhelm
   1971   "*Eidslon*." In <u>The New International Dictionary of Theology</u>. Ed. Colin Brown. 4 Vols. 2:284-286.

Murray, John
   1979   "First Epistle to the Corinthians." In <u>The New International Standard Bible Encyclopedia</u>. Vol. 1. Geoffrey W. Bromiley, ed. Pp. 774-779. Grand Rapids: William B. Eerdmans Publishing Company.
   1965   <u>The Epistle to the Romans</u>. The New International Commentary on the New Testament. F. F. Bruce, ed. Grand Rapids: William B. Eerdmans Publishing Company.

Myers Allen C.
   1979   "<u>Death</u>." In The International Standard Bible Encyclopedia. Vol 1. Geoffrey W. Bromiley, ed. Pp. 89-901. Grand Rapids: William B. Eerdmans Publishing Company.

Nacpil, Emerito
   1976   "A Gospel for the New Filipino." in <u>Asian Voices in Christian Theology</u>, Gerald H. Anderson, ed. Pp. 117-145. Maryknoll, NY: Orbis Books.

National Statistics Office
   2000   <u>Proclamation No. 28</u>. Manila: Malacañang.

Neo, Julma
   1975   "A Structure of the Faith Experience of Filipino Rural Catholics in the Light of the Constitution on Divine Revelation." M.A. thesis, Ateneo de Manila University.

Novilla, Manual C.
   1971   "Implications of the Traditional Beliefs and Practices Regarding Illness, Death, and Burial for Elementary Education in Alang-Alang, Leyte." M.A. Thesis, Divine Word University Tacloban City, Leyte.

Opena, Johnny
    2002   Personal interview with a researcher of the author, Palo, Leyte, April 9.

Pacayra, Romualda
    2001   Personal interview with the author's wife. Catbologan, Western Samar, November-December.

Pashley, Margaret
    2001   Personal interview with the author's wife. Tacloban City, Leyte, November 20.

Pal, Agaton
    1956   "A Philippine Barrio: A Study of Social Organization in Relation to Planned Cultural Change." Journal of Southeast Asian Studies 4(4): 333-486.

Petaller, Eliseo
    2001   Personal interview with the author. Catbologan, Western Samar, November 27.

Pieris, Aloysius
    1989   An Asian Theology of Liberation. Quezon City: Claretarian Publications. Cited in Leonardo N. Mercado. Inculturation and Filipino Theology. Manila: Divine Word Publications, 1992:19.

Ranon, Alan
    2001   Personal interview with the author's wife. Western Samar, November-December.

Scheans, D.J., Hutterer, Karl L. and Cherry, R.L.
    1970   "Some Oracion Tattoos From Samar." Leyte-Samar Studies 4 (1):29-45

Schreiter, Robert
    1985   Local Theologies. London: SCM Press, Ltd.

Schumaker, John
    1984   "Syncretism in Philippine Catholicism: Its Historical Causes." Philippine Studies 32: 251.

Schuman, Howard and Presser, Stanley
    1996   Questions and Answers in Attitude Surveys: Experiments on Question Form, Wording, and Context. Thousand Oaks, CA: Sage Publications.

Sirkin, R. Mark
    1999   Statistics for the Social Sciences. 2nd Edition. Thousand Oaks,

CA: Sage Publications.

Snider, Bill
    2003   Telephone conversation with the author, February 6.

Sogaard, Viggo
    1996   <u>Research in Church and Mission</u>. Pasadena, CA: William Carey Library.

Stamps, Donald ed.
    1992   <u>The Full Life Study Bible</u>. Grand Rapids: Zondervan Publishing Company.

Stauffer, Ethelbert
    1964   "*Eis.*" In <u>Theological Dictionary of the New Testament</u>. Vol 2. Gerhard Kittel, ed. Translated Geoffrey W. Bromiley. Grand Rapids: William B. Eerdmans Publishing Company.

Sumulat, Pedro
    2001   Personal interview with the author. Guiuan, Eastern Samar, December.

Squadra, Joseline
    2002   Personal inteview with a researcher of the author. Palo, Leyte, April 9.

Tate, Marvin E.
    1990   <u>Psalms 51-100</u>. Word Biblical Commentary, Vol 20. David A. Hubbard and Glenn W. Barker, eds. Dallas, TX: Word Books.

Teleron, Milagros R.
    1972   "The Function of Folk-Religious Rituals and Beliefs Related to the Life Cycle of the People of Barrio Puerto Bello, Municipality of Merida, Province of Leyte.: M.A. thesis, Silliman University.

Terian, Abraham
    1982   "Idol." In <u>The International Standard Bible Encyclopedia</u>. Vol 2. Geoffrey W. Bromiley, ed. Pp. 794-800. Grand Rapids: William B. Eerdmans Publishing Company.

Thiessen, Henry
    1979   <u>Lectures in Systematic Theology</u>. ed. Vernon D. Doerksen. Grand Rapids: William B. Eerdmans Publishing Company.

Tiongson, Nicanor G, ed.
    1994   <u>CCP Encyclopedia of the Arts</u>. Manila: Cultural Center of the Philippines.

Tiston, Rebecca
    1982   "The Tambalans of Northern Leyte." <u>Leyte-Samar Studies</u>. 16 (1):1-67.
    1977   "The Psychology of the Tambalan in Leyte." In <u>Filipino Religious Psychology</u>. Leonardo N. Mercado, ed. Pp. 22-35. Tacloban City: Divine Word University Publications.

Van Rheenen, Gailyn
    1991   <u>Communicating Christ in Animistic Contexts</u>. Grand Rapids: Baker Book House.

Villegas, Maria
    1968   "A Study of Traditional Beliefs and Practices in the Coastal Towns of Eastern Leyte and Their Educational Implications." M.A. Thesis, University of Santo Tomas Graduate School.

Wallace, Ronald S.
    1986   "Mediation." In <u>The International Standard Bible Encyclopedia</u>. Vol 3. Geoffrey W. Bromiley, ed. Pp. 299-305. Grand Rapids: William B. Eerdmans Publishing Company.

Wilkinson, John
    1998   <u>The Bible and Healing: A Medical and Theological Commentary</u>. Grand Rapids: William B. Eerdmans Publishing Company.

Williams, J. Rodman
    1996   Renewal Theology: <u>Systematic Theology From a Charismatic Perspective</u>. 3 Vols. Grand Rapids: Zondervan Publishing Company.

Wright, Gordon
    1984   <u>In Quest of Healing</u>. Springfield, MO: Gospel Publishing House.

Yambot, Efren, ed.
    1993   <u>Factbook Philippines</u>. Manila: Active Research Center.

Also by DAVE JOHNSON: LED BY THE SPIRIT

Available in the Philippines at

ICI Distribution Center
BBC Compound
Gov. I Santiago St.
Malinta, Valenzuela City 1405
(02) 292.8509; 294.6137 / www.iciphilippines.org

APTS Campus Bookstore
444 Ambuklao Rd
2600 Baguio City
www.apts.edu

And selected bookstores nationwide

Available outside the Philippines at
www.daveanddebbiejohnson.com

Asian Journal of Pentecostal Studies

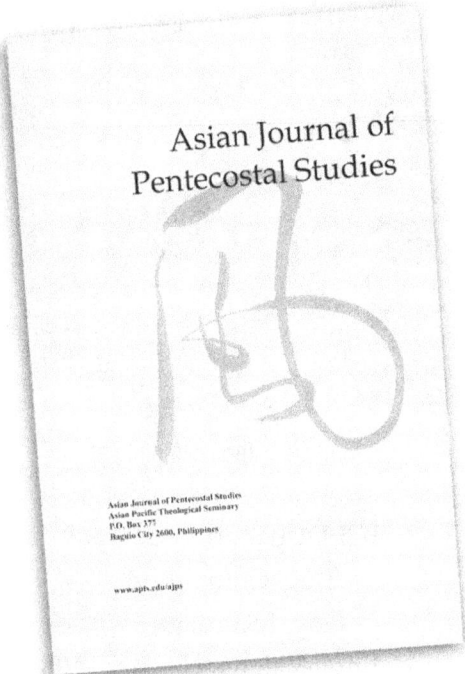

www.apts.edu

www.ingramcontent.com/pod-product-compliance
Lightning Source LLC
Chambersburg PA
CBHW070318230426
43663CB00011B/2178